PIANO · VOCAL

HOLLYWOOD MUSICALS YEAR·BY·YEAR

VOLUME 3
1949 TO 1955

The essays about each film are excerpted from the book *Hollywood Musicals
Year by Year* by author Stanley Green (Hal Leonard Corporation, 1990) with
additional text on recent movies by Richard Walters.

HAL·LEONARD™
CORPORATION
7777 W. BLUEMOUND RD. P.O. BOX 13819 MILWAUKEE, WI 53213

ISBN 0-7935-3208-6

Hollywood Musicals Year by Year 1949-1955
Index By Song Title

Hollywood Musicals Year by Year 1949-1955
Chronological Index

The Barkleys of Broadway

Music: Harry Warren, etc.
Lyrics: Ira Gershwin
Screenplay: Betty Comden & Adolph Green
Produced by: Arthur Freed for MGM
Directed by: Charles Walters
Choreography: Robert Alton, Hermes Pan (Fred Astaire uncredited)
Photography: Harry Stradling (Technicolor)
Cast: Fred Astaire, Ginger Rogers, Oscar Levant, Billie Burke, Jacques Francois, Gale Robbins, George Zucco, Hans Conried, Joyce Matthews, Lennie Hayton, Dee Turnell
Songs & instrumentals: "Swing Trot" (instrumental); "Sabre Dance" (Khatchaturian); "You'd Be Hard to Replace"; "Bouncin' the Blues" (instrumental); "My One and Only Highland Fling"; "A Weekend in the Country"; "Shoes with Wings On"; Piano Concerto in B-flat Minor (excerpt) (Tschaikowsky); "They Can't Take That Away from Me" (music: George Gershwin); "Manhattan Downbeat"
Released: May 1949; 109 minutes

Ginger Rogers and Fred Astaire doing the "Bouncin' the Blues" number during a rehearsal.

With *Easter Parade* one of the biggest moneymakers of 1948, producer Arthur Freed was quick to make plans for another show-business tale that would again costar Judy Garland and Fred Astaire. Since the previous movie had ended with a bickering vaudeville couple winning acclaim in their first Broadway show, it occurred to screenwriters Betty Comden and Adolph Green that a modern story could be woven around bickering married couple, Josh and Dinah Barkley, who have apparently been enjoying nothing but success as the musical theatre's answer to Alfred Lunt and Lynn Fontanne. The conflict in the film would center on the way they cope with the crisis—fortunately only temporary—of Dinah's deserting musicals in favor of heavy drama. (The writers even had Dinah appear in a play as Sarah Bernhardt and recite the "Marseillaise" in French!)

For the project, Freed brought together many of the same people who had worked with him on *Easter Parade*: director Charles Walters, choreographer Robert Alton, associate producer Roger Edens, director of photography Harry Stradling, art director Cedric Gibbons, and editor Albert Akst. For the songs, however, he turned to composer Harry Warren and lyricist Ira Gershwin for what would be the only project on which they ever worked together.

After rehearsals for *The Barkleys of Broadway* had already begun, Miss Garland's illness caused the actress to be absent so often that Freed was forced to replace her—which led him to Astaire's most celebrated dancing partner, Ginger Rogers. (It was their first film together in nine years and their tenth and final costarring appearance.) The cast change required alterations to both the script and the songs (no less than nine numbers were discarded), plus the addition of the interpolated George and Ira Gershwin ballad, "They Can't Take That Away from Me," which had been first sung by Fred to Ginger in *Shall We Dance*, and is here performed as a formal song-and-dance routine during a benefit show.

Among the film's memorable musical scenes are the seemingly spontaneous Astaire-Rogers rehearsal dance to the instrumental "Bouncin' the Blues"; Fred's solo "Shoes with Wings On," performed in a shoe-repair store with dozens of disembodied tapping shoes; and the Scottish duet, "My One and Only Highland Fling," burred by Fred and Ginger wearing tam-o'-shanters, kilts, and dour expressions. In Great Britain the movie was known as *The Gay Barkleys*.

Sountrak St. MGM/UA VC.

They Can't Take That Away from Me

FROM THE BARKLEYS OF BROADWAY

Music and Lyrics by GEORGE GERSHWIN
and IRA GERSHWIN

Our ro - mance won't end on a sor - row - ful note,

Though by to - mor - row you're gone; The song is end - ed,

but as the song - writ - er wrote, The mel - o - dy ling - ers

In the Good Old Summertime

Screenplay: Albert Hackett, Frances Goodrich, Van Tors
Produced by: Joe Pasternak for MGM
Directed by: Robert Z. Leonard
Choreography: Robert Alton
Photography: Harry Stradling (Technicolor)
Cast: Judy Garland, Van Johnson, S. Z. Sakall, Spring Byington, Clinton Sundberg, Buster Keaton, Marcia Van Dyke, Liza Minnelli
Songs: "In the Good Old Summertime" (George Evans-Ren Shields); "Meet Me Tonight in Dreamland" (Leo Friedman-Beth Whitson); "Put Your Arms Around Me, Honey" (Albert von Tilzer-Junie McCree); "Play That Barbershop Chord" (Lewis Muir-William Tracey); "I Don't Care" (Harry Sutton-Jean Lenox); "Merry Christmas" (Fred Spielman-Janice Torre)
Released: June 1949; 102 minutes

S. Z. Sakall, Van Johnson, and Judy Garland in Oberkugen's Music Store.

I*n the Good Old Summertime* began life as a Hungarian play, *Parfumerie* by Miklos Laszlo, which was first filmed in 1939 by Ernst Lubitsch as *The Shop Around the Corner* with Margaret Sullavan and James Stewart. (In 1963, the original version would be adapted as a Broadway musical, *She Loves Me*). For *In the Good Old Summertime* (actually, the film covers the period from summer to Christmas), the locale was changed from modern Budapest to Chicago after the turn of the century, and Maraczek's leather goods and novelty shop became Oberkugen's Music Store. The main story of two antagonistic shop clerks who anonymously carry on a romantic postal correspondence was retained, but the conflict caused by the store owner's unfaithful wife was changed to one caused when the owner's beloved Stradivarius is lent to a music student without his permission.

After pregnant June Allyson had to bow out of the film, Judy Garland was signed to star opposite Van Johnson. To give the movie an authentic period flavor, six of the songs dated from the century's first decade, though there was a new song, "Merry Christmas," inserted as something of a successor to "Have Youself a Merry Little Christmas." In the final scene showing the once battling shop clerks now happily married, their progeny was played by Miss Garland's own three-year-old daughter, Liza Minnelli.

MCA ST. MGM/UA VC.

In the Good Old Summertime

FROM IN THE GOOD OLD SUMMERTIME

Words by REN SHEILDS
Music by GEORGE EVANS

In the good old sum - mer -
time, _____ in the good old
sum - mer - time, _____ stroll - ing

through the shad - y lanes with your ba - by mine. You hold her hand and she holds yours and that's a

Neptune's Daughter

Music & lyrics: Frank Loesser
Screenplay: Dorothy Kingsley
Produced by: Jack Cummings for MGM
Directed by: Edward Buzzell
Choreography: Jack Donohue
Photography: Charles Rosher (Technicolor)
Cast: Esther Williams, Red Skelton, Ricardo
Montalban, Betty Garrett, Keenan Wynn,
Xavier Cugat Orch., Mel Blanc
Songs: "I Love Those Men"; "My Heart Beats
Faster"; "Baby, It's Cold Outside"
Released: June 1949; 93 minutes

Red Skelton and Betty Garrett.

With theatre rental earnings of $3.45 million, *Neptune's Daughter* was not only among the biggest draws of 1949, it was also the most popular of the 18 splashy musicals in which Esther Williams appeared. In the movie, Hollywood's only female natant star plays an amateur swimming champion who becomes a successful swimsuit designer and manufacturer. When a South American polo team, led by Ricardo Montalban, comes to New York, Esther stages a fashion show in and around the polo club's pool. Her man-hungry sister, Betty Garrett, mistakes the club's masseur, Red Skelton, for Montalban and Esther is angry at Montalban for breaking her sister's heart. Take it from there. The musical highlight of the film is the duet, "Baby, It's Cold Outside," which had originally been written by composer-lyricist Frank Loesser as a song that he and his wife could sing at parties. Curiously, just before it is sung in the picture, Montalban urges Miss Williams to stay with him on "this warm summer evening."

MGM/UA VC.

1949

Baby, It's Cold Outside
FROM THE MOTION PICTURE NEPTUNE'S DAUGHTER

By FRANK LOESSER

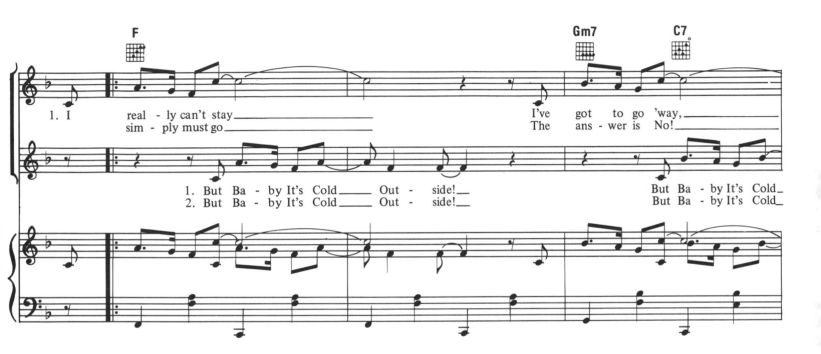

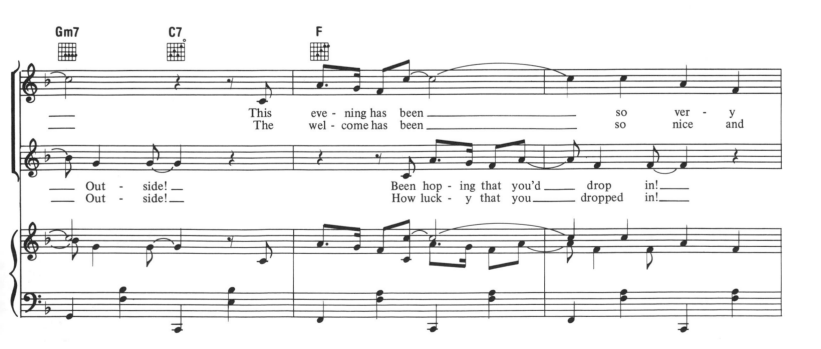

neigh-bors might think _____ Say, What's in this drink? _____
got to get home _____ Say, lend me a comb _____

But, ba - by, it's bad ____ out there ____ No cabs to be had ____
But, ba - by, you'd freeze ____ out there ____ It's up to your knees ____

____ out there ____ I wish I knew how _____ to break the
____ out there ____ You've real - ly been grand _____ but don't you

Your eyes are like star - light now ____
I thrill when you touch ____ my hand ____

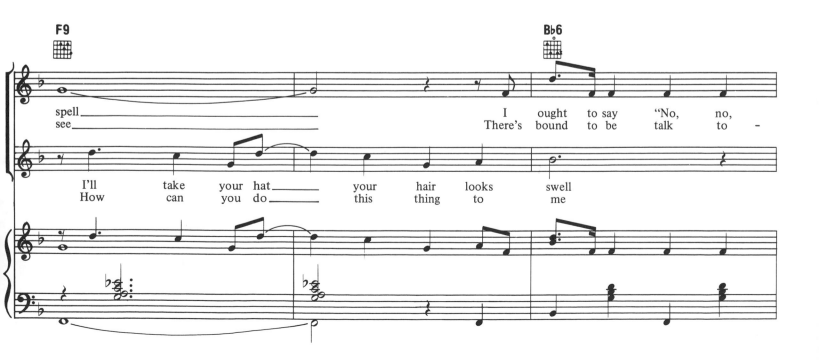

spell _____ I ought to say "No, no,
see _____ There's bound to be talk to -

I'll take your hat _____ your hair looks swell
How can you do ____ this thing looks to me

no, Sir!"___ At least I'm gon - na say that I tried I
mor - row.___ At least there will be plen - ty im - plied I

Mind if I move in clos - er?___ What's the sense of hurt - ing my pride
Think of my life - long sor - row___ If you caught pneu - mo - nia and died__

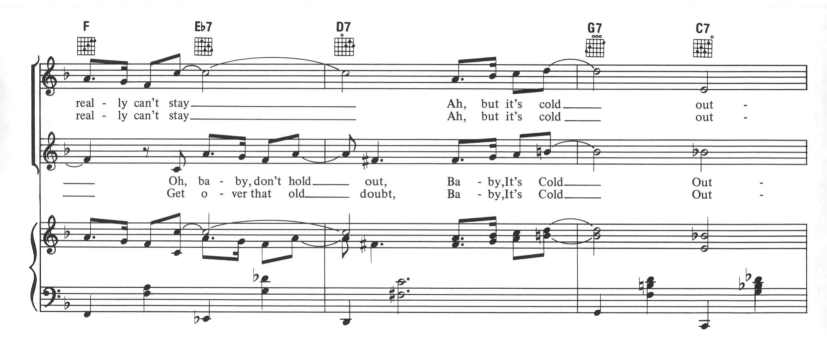

real - ly can't stay___ Ah, but it's cold___ out -
real - ly can't stay___ Ah, but it's cold___ out -

___ Oh, ba - by, don't hold___ out, Ba - by, It's Cold___ Out -
___ Get o - ver that old___ doubt, Ba - by, It's Cold___ Out -

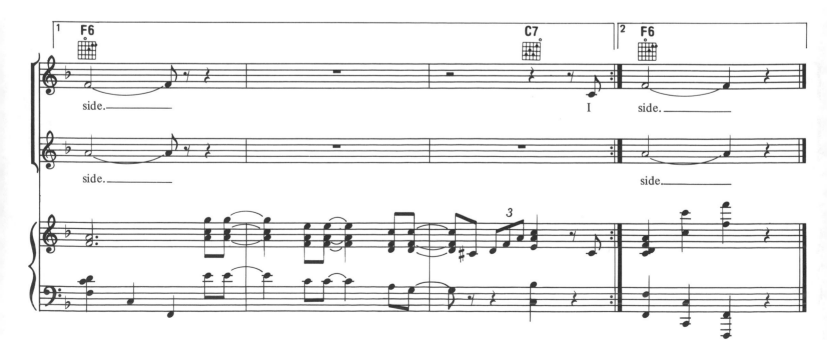

side.___ I side.___

side.___ side.___

CINDERELLA

Music & lyrics: Al Hoffman, Jerry Livingston, Mack David

Screenplay: Kenneth Anderson, Ted Sears, Homer Brightman, Joe Rinaldi, William Peet, Harry Reeves, Winston Hibler, Erdman Penner

Produced by: Walt Disney (released by RKO Radio)

Directed by: Wilfred Jackson, Hamilton Luske, Clyde Geronimi (Technicolor)

Voices: Ilene Woods, William Phipps, Eleanor Audley, Rhoda Williams, Lucille Bliss, Verna Felton, Luis Van Rooten

Songs: "Bibbidi Bobbidi Boo"; "So This Is Love"; "A Dream Is a Wish Your Heart Makes"; "Cinderella"; "Sing, Sweet Nightingale"; "The Work Song"

Released: December 1949; 74 minutes

According to the most recent Guinness Book on the movies, *Cinderella* has had more screen versions than any other story. Five of these productions have been musicals—*First Love* (1939) with Deanna Durbin; the Walt Disney cartoon feature *Cinderella* (1949); *The Glass Slipper* (1955) with Leslie Caron; *CinderFella* (1960) with Jerry Lewis; and *The Slipper and the Rose* (1976) with Gemma Craven. Disney's version, whose latest reissue was in 1987, has been by far the most successful (at latest count, it has taken in $41 million in domestic theatre rental fees). The cartoon follows the general fairytale formula established by *Snow White and the Seven Dwarfs*, while adding new characters such as Cinderella's resourceful rodent chums, Jacques and Gus, who get the other mice to make a ball gown for our heroine. Though its exact origins are obscure, *Cinderella* as we know it today was first written by Charles Perrault, a 17th Century French writer who called it *Cendrillon ou la Petite Pantoufle de Vair*, though through the years the slipper of squirrel fur (vair) was changed to one of glass (verre).

Disney VC.

1949

A Dream Is a Wish Your Heart Makes

FROM WALT DISNEY'S CINDERELLA

Words and Music by MACK DAVID,
AL HOFFMAN and JERRY LIVINGSTON

ON THE TOWN

Music: Leonard Bernstein*; Roger Edens**
Lyrics & screenplay: Betty Comden & Adolph Green
Produced by: Arthur Freed for MGM
Directors-choreographers: Gene Kelly & Stanley
    Donen
Photography: Harold Rosson (Technicolor)
Cast: Gene Kelly, Frank Sinatra, Betty Garrett, Ann Miller,
    Jules Munshin, Vera-Ellen, Florence Bates, Alice Pearce,
    Hans Conried, Carol Haney, George Meader, Bea
    Benaderet
Songs: "I Feel Like I'm Not Out of Bed Yet"*; "New York,
    New York"*; "Miss Turnstiles"* ballet (instrumental);
    "Prehistoric Man"**; "Come Up to My Place"*; "Main
    Street"**; "You're Awful"**; "On the Town"**; "Count on
    Me"**; "A Day in New York"* ballet (instrumental)
Released: December 1949; 98 minutes

The "Count on Me" number performed by Betty Garrett, Ann Miller, Gene Kelly, Jules Munshin, Frank Sinatra, and Alice Pearce.

A ballet titled *Fancy Free* was the genesis of *On the Town*, the successful 1944 stage musical that served to introduce Broadway to the talents of composer Leonard Bernstein, lyricists-librettists Betty Comden and Adolph Green, and choreographer Jerome Robbins. Its tale focuses on three sailors on 24-hour shore leave in New York, the sights they see, and the three girls they meet and fall for before it is time to return to their ship. The story may have been slight—and slightly familiar—but the treatment was so inventive, both musically and choreographically, that the show played an influential role in the development of the American musical theatre.

For the screen, producer Arthur Freed put Gene Kelly and Frank Sinatra back in the sailor uniforms they had worn in *Anchors Aweigh* (which had also been about gobs on leave trying to pick up girls) and added Jules Munshin and Betty Garrett from *Take Me Out to the Ball Game* (with Miss Garrett again playing a boy-crazy girl chasing a girl-shy Sinatra). Vera-Ellen and Ann Miller rounded out the sextet as the girls fancied by Kelly and Munshin. The first film co-directed and choreograhed by Gene Kelly and Stanley Donen, *On the Town* utilized dance as a major component of the action in ways that had never before been attempted on the screen. It marked the first movie to have a musical sequence shot on location on New York, (the exuberant "New York, New York" number) and there was an imaginative ballet for Vera-Ellen as the winner of the subway's "Miss Turnstiles" competition. (Kelly would create a similar dance for Leslie Caron in *An American in Paris* two years later.) There was also a joyous routine atop the Empire State Building (actually filmed in Culver City), though the extended "Day in New York" ballet unnecessarily repeated the movie's plot.

Comden and Green were assigned to write the screenplay, but because Freed did not like it, Bernstein's score was limited to three songs and two ballets, with the rest of it replaced by five numbers written by Roger Edens and Comden and Green. Of the original Broadway cast, only Alice Pearce was engaged to recreate her role as Miss Garrett's sniffling roommate. The last of the three Kelly-Sinatra movies, *On the Town* placed among the box office winners of 1950.

Five years later, as something of a sequel, *It's Always Fair Weather*, also written by Comden and Green, took up the subject of a New York reunion of three army buddies played by Kelly, Dan Dailey and Michael Kidd, with Cyd Charisse and Dolores Gray in the leading female roles.

DRG (studio cast LP). MGM/UA VC.

New York, New York
FROM ON THE TOWN

Words by BETTY COMDEN and ADOLPH GREEN
Music by LEONARD BERNSTEIN

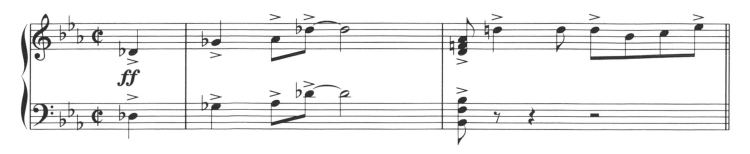

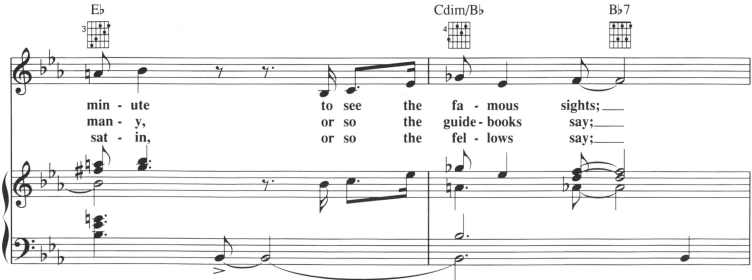

We've got____ one day____ here, and not an-oth-er
The fam-ous plac-___es to vis-___it are so
Man-hat-tan wom-___en are dressed in silk and

min-ute to see the fa-mous sights;____
man-y, or so the guide-books say;____
sat-in, or so the fel-lows say;____

Frank Sinatra, Gene Kelly, and Jules Munshin.

Take Me Out to the Ball Game

Music: Roger Edens, etc.
Lyrics: Betty Comden & Adolph Green, etc.
Screenplay: Harry Tugend & George Wells
Produced by: Arthur Freed for MGM
Directed by: Busby Berkeley
Choreography: Gene Kelly & Stanley Donen
Photography: George Folsey (Technicolor)
Cast: Frank Sinatra, Esther Williams, Gene Kelly, Betty Garrett, Edward Arnold, Jules Munshin, Blackburn Twins, Sally Forrest
Songs: "Take Me Out to the Ball Game" (Albert von Tilzer-Jack Norworth); "Yes, Indeedy"; "O'Brien to Ryan to Goldberg"; "The Right Girl for Me"; "It's Fate Baby, It's Fate" (lyric: Roger Edens); "The Hat My Father Wore upon St. Patrick's Day" (Jean Schwartz-William Jerome)
Released: April 1949; 93 minutes

Gene Kelly and Frank Sinatra may have doffed their *Anchors Aweigh* sailor suits in favor of baseball uniforms in *Take Me Out to the Ball Game*, but they still portrayed the same basic characters of brashy Gene and bashful Frank. In the turn-of-the-century tale (from a story dreamed up by Kelly and Stanley Donen), they play shortstop and second baseman for a professional ball team known as the Wolves, have a separate career as vaudevillians during the off-season, and spend much of their time clowning with first baseman Jules Munshin (in a part originally intended for baseball manager Leo Durocher). At their Sarasota training camp, the Wolves find themselves with a new owner in the unlikely person of Esther Williams (who replaced first Kathryn Grayson then Judy Garland), a bit of casting that required both a new screenplay and even a new songwriting team . Romantic complications—which really weren't too complicated—involve man-hungry Betty Garrett chasing Sinatra who loves Williams who loves Kelly. The movie was retitled *Everybody's Cheering in Great Britain*.

Curtain Calls ST. MGM/UA VC.

Take Me Out to the Ball Game

FROM TAKE ME OUT TO THE BALL GAME

Words by JACK NORWORTH
Music by ALBERT von TILZER

Spirited Waltz

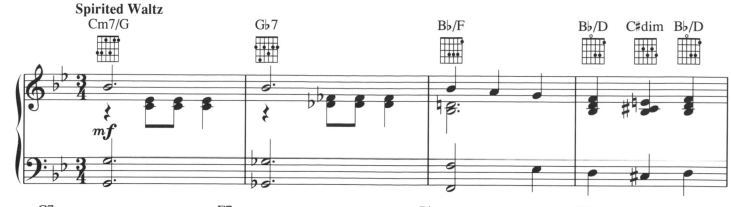

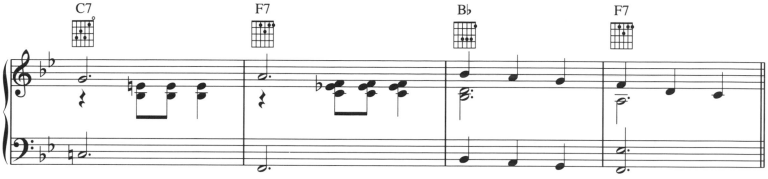

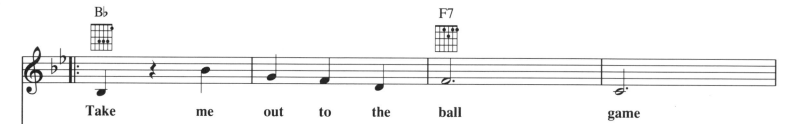

Take me out to the ball game

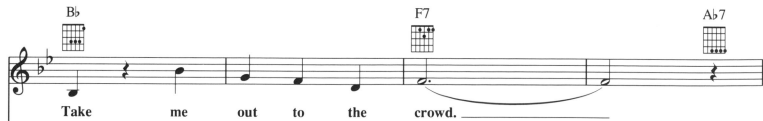

Take me out to the crowd. _____

ANNIE GET YOUR GUN

Music & lyrics: Irving Berlin
Screenplay: Sidney Sheldon
Produced by: Arthur Freed for MGM
Directed by: George Sidney
Choreography: Robert Alton
Photography: Charles Rosher (Technicolor)
Cast: Betty Hutton, Howard Keel, Louis Calhern, J. Carrol Naish, Edward Arnold, Keenan Wynn, Benay Venuta, Clinton Sundberg, Andre Charlot, Mae Clarke, Chief Yowlachie, Bradley Mora, Diana Dick, Susan Odin, Eleanor Brown
Songs: "Colonel Buffalo Bill"; "Doin' What Comes Natur'lly"; "The Girl That I Marry"; "You Can't Get a Man with a Gun"; "There's No Business Like Show Business"; "They Say It's Wonderful"; "My Defenses Are Down"; "I'm an Indian, Too"; "I Got the Sun in the Morning"; "Anything You Can Do"
Released: April 1950; 107 minutes

Betty Hutton singing "Doin' What Comes Natur'lly."

Ethel Merman may have been the Queen of Broadway Musicals and *Annie Get Your Gun* may have given her her longest reign, but when MGM bought the screen rights to the 1946 smash (at a record price of $700,000), the studio had no other star in mind but Judy Garland. After recording all her songs and performing before the camera for almost two months under Busby Berkeley's direction, Miss Garland, as she had during the preparation of *The Barkleys of Broadway*, became too sick to continue. Metro put her on suspension, considered Betty Garrett as her replacement, but ultimately gave the plum role of sharpshooter Annie Oakley to Betty Hutton, thus becoming her only musical assignment away from Paramount. (The MGM brass had most likely seen her in *Incendiary Blonde*, in which, as Texas Guinan, Miss Hutton first wins acclaim in a Wild West show.) Following a five-month delay, shooting resumed with two other major changes—George Sidney replaced Berkeley as director and Louis Calhern replaced Frank Morgan as Buffalo Bill following Morgan's death. *Annie Get Your Gun* also marked the screen debut of Howard Keel, who won the leading male role over John Raitt.

The biggest box office musical success of 1950, the movie version retained ten of the 15 songs in Irving Berlin's original hit-filled score, though "Moonshine Lullaby" and "Let's Go West Again," which were supposed to be in the film were casualties, and "Doin' What Comes Natur'lly" was both laundered and shortened. Adapted from the libretto by Dorothy and Herbert Fields, Sidney Sheldon's screen treatment was a faithful transference that also took full advantage of the medium, as in the spectacular "There's No Business Like Show Business" finale.

In the tale, which made no attempt at historical accuracy, tomboyish hillbilly marksman Annie Oakley, smitten by Frank Butler, the star attraction of Buffalo Bill's Wild West Show, joins the show and not only becomes Frank's rival but even boasts that anything he can do she can do better. Annie, however, stifles her competitiveness and bows to male chauvinism by purposely losing a marksmanship contest with Frank—and thereby winning her man.

The success of *Annie Get Your Gun* was the catalyst for Warners' 1953 musical, *Calamity Jane*, a pale variation starring Doris Day and, again, Howard Keel (as Wild Bill Hickock). In 1935, RKO Radio had released a nonmusical film, *Annie Oakley*, with Barbara Stanwyck and Preston Foster as the shooting stars.

MGM ST.

I Got the Sun in the Morning

FROM ANNIE GET YOUR GUN

Words and Music by
IRVING BERLIN

Tak-ing stock of what I have and what I have-n't, what do I find? The things I've got will keep me sat-is-fied.

Sun - shine _____ gives me a love - ly day. _____

_____ Moon - light _____ gives me the milk -

- y way. _____ Got no check - books,

got no banks, _____ still I'd like _____ to ex -

Summer Stock

Music: Harry Warren, etc.
Lyrics: Mack Gordon, etc.
Screenplay: George Wells, Sy Gomberg
Produced by: Joe Pasternak for MGM
Directed by: Charles Walters
Choreography: Nick Castle (Gene Kelly, Charles Walters uncredited)
Photography: Robert Planck (Technicolor)
Cast: Judy Garland, Gene Kelly, Eddie Bracken, Gloria DeHaven, Marjorie Main, Phil Silvers, Ray Collins, Carleton Carpenter, Hans Conried, Carol Haney
Songs: "Happy Harvest"; "If You Feel Like Singing, Sing"; "You Wonderful You" (lyric: Jack Brooks, Saul Chaplin); "Friendly Star"; "Heavenly Music" (Chaplin); "Get Happy" (Harold Arlen-Ted Koehler)
Released: August 1950; 108 minutes

Gene Kelly and Judy Garland dancing to "You Wonderful You."

The story is all about a theatrical troupe of young Broadway hopefuls having all kinds of problems trying out a new show in a Connecticut barn—so let's page Mickey and Judy! That, at least, was the original plan of producer Joe Pasternak, but he had second thoughts because the Judy Garland-Gene Kelly combination seemed like a stronger box office bet. And so the couple appeared together for the third and last time in a film that also happened to be Miss Garland's 27th and final picture at MGM. In this unpretentious, predictable tale, Judy played the farmer on whose land the barn is located and Gene the leader of the acting company that Judy, against her will, has allowed to stay on her property.

The stars' duet "You Wonderful You" was a highlight as was Kelly's dance on a newspaper covering the barn's squeaky floor. Judy's health problems caused so many delays that the shooting schedule was forced to run over eight months. They were also responsible for her being noticeably overweight. Two months after filming had stopped, however, when she returned to do the classic "Get Happy" number, Judy had shed 20 pounds and was back to her normal figure. The film's title—something of a misnomer since it was not really about a summer stock company—was changed in Great Britain to *If You Feel Like Singing*.

CBS ST. MGM/UA VC.

Get Happy
FROM SUMMER STOCK

Lyrics by TED KOEHLER
Music by HAROLD ARLEN

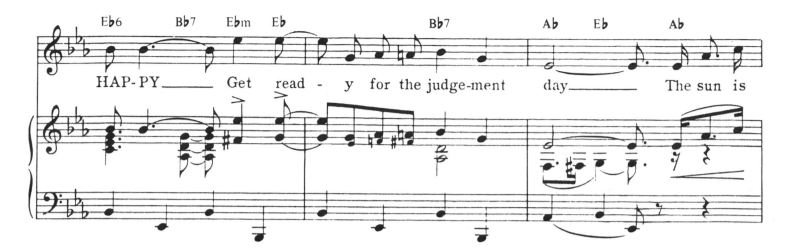

HAP-PY _____ Get read - y for the judge-ment day _____ The sun is

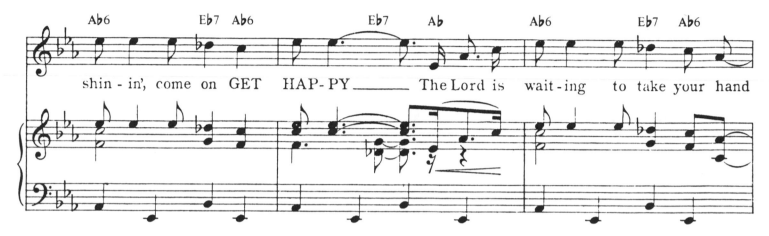

shin - in', come on GET HAP-PY _____ The Lord is wait-ing to take your hand

_____ Shout Hal-le - lu-jah! come on, GET HAP-PY _____ We're go -

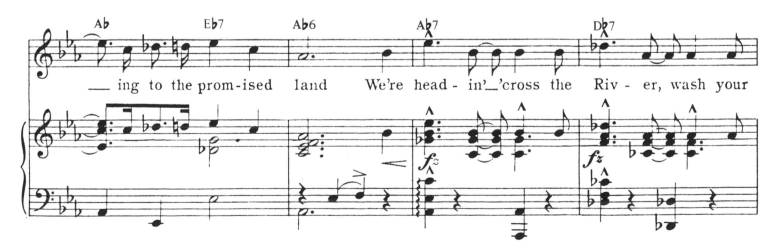

_ ing to the prom-ised land We're head - in'_'cross the Riv - er, wash your

sins 'way in the tide. It's all so peace-ful on the oth-er

side___ For-get your troub-les and just GET HAP-PY___ You bet-ter

chase all your cares a-way___ Shout Hal-le-lu-jah! come on, GET

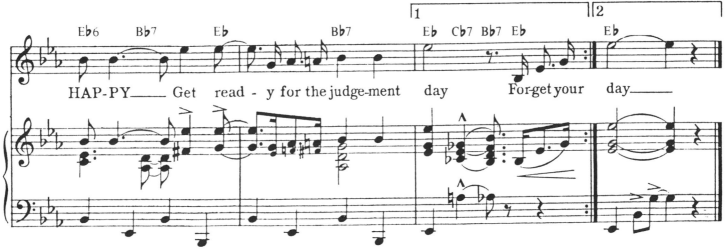

HAP-PY___ Get read-y for the judge-ment day   For-get your   day___

THREE LITTLE WORDS

Music: Harry Ruby, etc.
Lyrics: Bert Kalmar, etc.
Screenplay: George Wells
Produced by: Jack Cummings for MGM
Directed by: Richard Thorpe
Choreography: Hermes Pan (Fred Astaire uncredited)
Photography: Harry Jackson (Technicolor)
Cast: Fred Astaire, Red Skelton, Vera-Ellen, Arlene Dahl, Keenan Wynn, Gale Robbins, Gloria DeHaven, Phil Regan, Debbie Reynolds, Carleton Carpenter, Harry Barris, Harry Ruby
Songs: "Where Did You Get That Girl?" (music: Harry Puck); "My Sunny Tennessee" (with Herman Ruby); "So Long, Oo-Long"; "Who's Sorry Now?" (with Ted Snyder); "Nevertheless"; "All Alone Monday"; "I Wanna Be Loved by You" (music with Herbert Stothart); "Thinking of You"; "I Love You So Much"; "Three Little Words"
Released: July 1950; 103 minutes

Hollywood had just about run out of major Broadway songwriters to provide catalogues upon which some semblance of biographical fact and fiction could be strung, when MGM decided to film the life story of Bert Kalmar and Harry Ruby. In dealing with these prolific, though relatively obscure, writers, producer Jack Cummings avoided the all-star, elaborate approach in favor of concentrating on the skills, both musical and comedic, of its two stars, Fred Astaire and Red Skelton, as well as on the pleasures of the 15 numbers paraded throughout the film. Among them was "I Wanna Be Loved by You," for which Debbie Reynolds (as Helen Kane) did the mouthing to Miss Kane's own boop-boop-a-doop dubbing. The movie also gave Astaire a new dancing partner, Vera-Ellen, though it limited his terpsichorean efforts by having Kalmar, depicted as a vaudeville hoofer, break his leg about a quarter of the way through the film, thus forcing him to become a full-time lyricist. (Actually, the real Kalmer had a magic and comedy act.) The plot is primarily concerned with Kalmar's efforts to keep Ruby away from gold-digging females by shipping him off to a Florida baseball training camp to be with his beloved Washington Senators. The men squabble, break up, and come back together to accidentally write one of their biggest hits, "Three Little Words."

MGM ST. MGM/UA VC.

Who's Sorry Now

FROM THREE LITTLE WORDS

Words by BERT KALMER and HARRY RUBY
Music by TED SNYDER

An American in Paris

Music: George Gershwin
Lyrics: Ira Gershwin
Screenplay: Alan Jay Lerner
Produced by: Arthur Freed for MGM
Directed by: Vincente Minnelli
Choreography: Gene Kelly
Photography: Alfred Gilks, John Alton (Technicolor)
Cast: Gene Kelly, Leslie Caron, Oscar Levant, Georges
 Guetary, Nina Foch, Benny Carter Orch., Andre Charisse,
 Eugene Borden, Martha Bamattre, Ann Codee, Dudley
 Field Malone
Songs & instrumentals: "Embraceable You"; "By
 Strauss"; "I Got Rhythm"; "Tra-La-La"; "Love Is Here to
 Stay"; "I'll Build a Stairway to Paradise" (lyric with B.G.
 DeSylva); "Piano Concerto in F" (third movement); " 'S
 Wonderful"; "An American in Paris" (ballet)
Released: August 1951; 113 minutes

Gene Kelly and Leslie Caron in the ballet.

He had no story or score, but producer Arthur Freed was certain of three things: the movie would be about an American in Paris, it would be called *An American in Paris*, and it would somehow use the Gershwin orchestral suite as part of the story. The next logical step was to have an all-Gershwin score and Freed, joined by director Vincente Minnelli and his staff, came up with about a dozen songs plus the third movement of the Piano Concerto in F. Once it was decided to create a ballet as the movie's climax, Gene Kelly became the logical choice for the title role.

Screenwriter Alan Jay Lerner devised an accommodating tale about a carefree, impecunious painter, former GI Jerry Mulligan (Kelly), who needs no more than one look to fall hopelessly in love with pert young Parisian Lise Bourvier (French ballet dancer Leslie Caron, then 19, in her film debut). Lise somehow finds herself succumbing to the aggressively gauche American—particularly when they dance to "Love Is Here to Stay" on a Seine River embankment but there is a complication: she is engaged to an older man, popular music hall singer Henri Baurel (Georges Guetary, who was actually two-and-a-half years younger than Kelly). Another complication arises when wealthy American Milo Richards (Nina Foch), who has taken a fancy to Jerry, offers to set him up in an elegant studio and introduce him to all the right people. (This situation was doubtlessly prompted by the Broadway musical *Pal Joey*, in which Kelly had first won recognition.) Through a mutual friend, composer Adam Cook (Oscar Levant), Jerry and Henri become acquainted without being aware that each loves the same girl. At the film's end, of course, Jerry wins Lise with Henri's blessing.

When Miss Foch was forced to miss work for a few days because of illness, the delay gave Kelly time to concentrate on the *American in Paris* ballet. He came up with the idea of having Jerry, brooding about his lost love, think about Paris and Lise and what they both mean to him, with the dance evolving as Jerry's way of expressing his varied emotions as he pursues Lise throughout the city. Because Jerry is an artist, each section of Paris is shown in the style of a famous painter—Dufy for the Place de la Concorde, Renoir for the Pont Neut, Utrillo for Montmartre, Rousseau for the zoo, Van Gogh for the Place de l'Opera, and Toulouse Lautrec for the Moulin Rouge. Lasting 17 minutes, the ballet took one month to shoot and cost $542,000.

Initially, Kelly wanted to film the musical sequences in Paris, but economic considerations forced Freed to shoot everything in Culver City. Despite forebodings that audiences wouldn't sit still for the ballet finale, *An American in Paris* placed high among the top money makers of 1951.

CBS ST MGM/UA VC.

1951

I'll Build a Stairway to Paradise

FROM AN AMERICAN IN PARIS

Words by B.G. DeSYLVA and IRA GERSHWIN
Music by GEORGE GERSHWIN

Animato

All you Preach-ers   Who de-light in pan-ning the

danc-ing teach-ers   Let me tell you there are a   lot of fea-tures

Show Boat

Music: Jerome Kern
Lyrics: Oscar Hammerstein II
Screenplay: John Lee Mahin
Produced by: Arthur Freed for MGM
Directed by: George Sidney
Choreography: Robert Alton
Photography: Charles Rosher (Technicolor)
Cast: Kathryn Grayson, Ava Gardner, Howard Keel, Joe E. Brown, Marge & Gower Champion, Robert Sterling, Agnes Moorehead, Leif Erickson, William Warfield, Regis Toomey, Fuzzy Knight, Chick Chandler
Songs: "Make Believe"; "Can't Help Lovin' Dat Man"; "I Might Fall Back on You"; "Ol' Man River"; "You Are Love"; "Why Do I Love You?"; "Bill" (lyric with P.G. Wodehouse); "Life upon the Wicked Stage"; "After the Ball" (Charles K. Harris)
Released: June 1951; 108 minutes

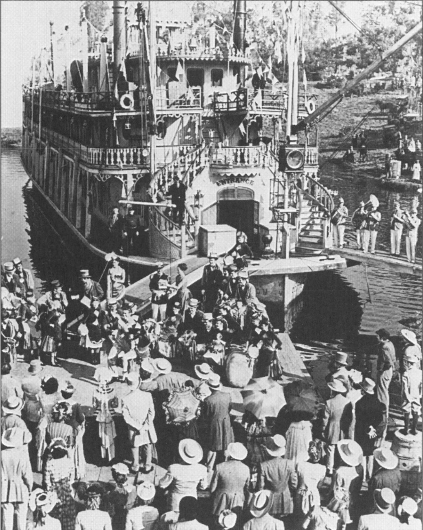

Show Boat. The *Cotton Blossom* comes to town.
The *Cotton Blossom* comes to town.

Not counting the abridgement in *Till the Clouds Roll By* (which also featured Kathryn Grayson), there have been three movie versions of the 1927 landmark Broadway production. During the first part of the 1951 adaptation, the script keeps close to the original Oscar Hammerstein libretto, including the love-at-first-sight meeting between Magnolia Hawks and riverboat gambler Gaylord Ravenal, the revelation that the showboat's star attraction, Julie La Verne, is part Negro and must leave the company, and Magnolia and Gay's marriage and their move to Chicago. Then the dramatic structure is considerably tightened by having Ravenal, now penniless, walk out on Magnolia while she is pregnant, and by having Magnolia, after singing in a Chicago night club on New Year's Eve, return with her father to the show boat to bring up her daughter (in the original, both she and daughter become musical-comedy stars on Broadway). Instead of waiting some 20 years until their accidental reunion, Magnolia and Gay are separated only about four years, and it is the tragic Julie who plays a crucial role in bringing them together. Initially, either Judy Garland or Dinah Shore seemed set for the role of Julie, but the part went to Ava Gardner (with her songs dubbed by Annette Warren, though the "soundtrack" album used Miss Gardner's voice).

CBS ST. MGM/UA VC.

1951

Ol' Man River

FROM SHOW BOAT

Lyrics by OSCAR HAMMERSTEIN II
Music by JEROME KERN

The Great Caruso

Jarmila Novotna, Mario Lanza, and Ian Wolfe meeting at the Metropolitan Opera House.

Screenplay: Sonia Levien & William Ludwig
Produced by: Joe Pasternak for MGM
Directed by: Richard Thorpe, Peter Herman Adler
Photography: Joseph Ruttenberg (Technicolor)
Cast: Mario Lanza, Ann Blyth, Dorothy Kirsten, Jarmila Novotna, Richard Hageman, Carl Benton Reid, Eduard Franz, Ludwig Donath, Mae Clarke, Ian Wolfe
Songs & arias: "La donna e mobile" (Verdi); "Celeste Aida" (Verdi); "Torna a Surriento" (DeCurtis); "O Paradiso" (Verdi); "Che gelida manina" (Puccini); "Vesti la Giubba" (Leoncavallo); "Ave Maria" (Bach-Gounod); "The Loveliest Night of the Year" (Juventino Rosas, Irving Aaronson-Paul Francis Webster); "Sextet" (Donizetti); "M'Appari" (Flotow); " 'Tis the Last Rose of Summer" (Thomas Moore)
Released: April 1951; 109 minutes

Mario Lanza appeared in only seven films and dubbed the soundtrack of an eighth (*The Student Prince*), but so great was his appeal that the robust, temperamental tenor did more to popularize opera than any other movie star. Lanza's biggest hit, the sugar-coated biography of the legendary opera singer, traces Enrico Caruso's story from his humble beginnings in Naples, through his idyllic marriage to a New York socialite (there is no mention of a previous common-law wife and their two sons, nor of Caruso's notorious womanizing), to his death of pleurisy at the age of 48 (Lanza himself died of a heart attack at 38). The ancient Mexican waltz known as "Over the Waves," usually associated with performing seals, was revised for the film and called "The Loveliest Night of the Year." Though sung by Ann Blyth as Mrs. Caruso, the song became a hit only after Lanza recorded it.

An Italian screen biography, *Enrico Caruso, Legend of a Voice*, with Ermanno Randi, was released the same year as *The Great Caruso*. The American film was followed by three other Hollywood biographies of opera stars: *So This Is Love* (1953), with Kathryn Grayson as Grace Moore (Miss Moore had played Jenny Lind in her 1930 biography, *A Lady's Morals*); *Melba* (1953), with Patrice Munsel as Nellie Melba; and *Interrupted Melody* (1955), with Eleanor Parker (with the voice of Eileen Farrell) as Marjorie Lawrence.

RCA ST. MGM/UA VC.

Vesti la Giubba

FROM THE GREAT CARUSO

Words and Music by
RUGGIERO LEONCAVALLO

gliac - cio!
gliac - cio!

On with your clown smock, On your
Ve - sti la giub - ba e la

face dab the pow - der,   The peo - ple pay you to have an eve - ning's fun.____
fac - cia in - fa - ri - na.   La gen - te pa - ga e ri - der vuo - le qua.____

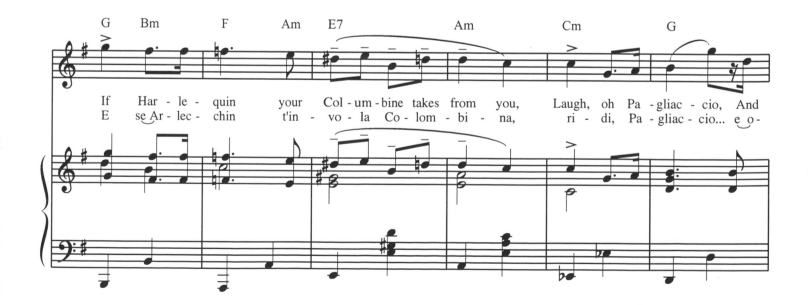

If Har - le - quin   your Col - um - bine takes from you,   Laugh, oh Pa - gliac - cio, And
E se Ar - lec - chin   t'in - vo - la Co - lom - bi - na,   ri - di, Pa - gliac - cio... e o-

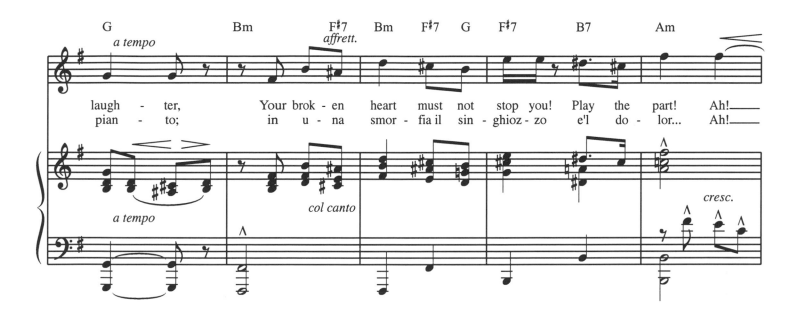

Am6   Em   B7   E

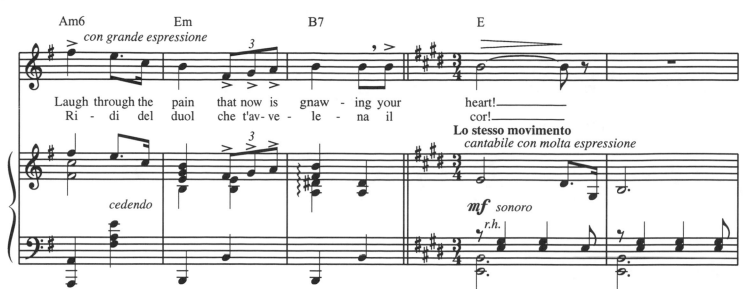

Laugh through the pain that now is gnaw - ing your heart!_____
Ri - di del duol che t'av-ve - le - na il cor!_____

Lo stesso movimento
cantabile con molta espressione

cedendo

mf sonoro
r.h.

cresc. sempre

f

poco rit. con dolore
p

rianimando

rit. *ed accentato molto*

marcato il canto
r.h.

Hans Christian Andersen

Music & lyrics: Frank Loesser
Screenplay: Moss Hart
Produced by: Samuel Goldwyn (released by RKO Radio)
Directed by: Charles Vidor
Choreography: Roland Petit
Photography: Harry Stradling (Technicolor)
Cast: Danny Kaye, Farley Granger, Jeanmaire, Joey Walsh, Erik
  Bruhn, Roland Petit
Songs: "The King's New Clothes"; "I'm Hans Christian Andersen";
  "Wonderful Copenhagen"; "Thumbelina"; "The Ugly Duckling";
  "Anywhere I Wander"; "The Inch Worm"; "No Two People"
Released: November 1952; 120 minutes

Danny Kaye singing the tale of "The King's New Clothes" to the children of Odense.

It took five years and 21 scripts before producer Samuel Goldwyn gave his approval to go ahead with the musical about Hans Christian Andersen—and then he ran into trouble with the Danish government for distorting the writer's life. Actually, the Moss Hart screenplay made no attempt at biographical accuracy, and the Danes were mollified when the movie was preceded by the explanation that it was "a fairy tale about a great spinner of fairy tales." With a subdued Danny Kaye in the title role, the plot, set in 1830, tells of a cobbler who entertains children in his native Odense by spinning stories, much to the displeasure of town officials. Andersen takes off for Copenhagen where he makes shoes for a ballerina (Jeanmaire), with whom he falls hopelessly in love and for whom he writes a 17-minute ballet, "The Little Mermaid." Back home in Odense the heartsick storyteller at last wins the appreciation of all his neighbors. More important to the success of the film than its somewhat downbeat script were the four ballets (comprising some 25% of the footage) and the imaginative Frank Loesser score, half of which was based on Andersen's fairy tales. Goldwyn's most lavish production to date, *Hans Christian Andersen* was one of the leading box office attractions of 1953.

A stage variation—which used the songs but not the script—opened in London in 1974 under the title *Hans Andersen*. Tommy Steele had the starring role.

Decca (Kaye LP). Nelson VC.

1952

No Two People

FROM THE MOTION PICTURE HANS CHRISTIAN ANDERSEN

By FRANK LOESSER

Medium Schottische

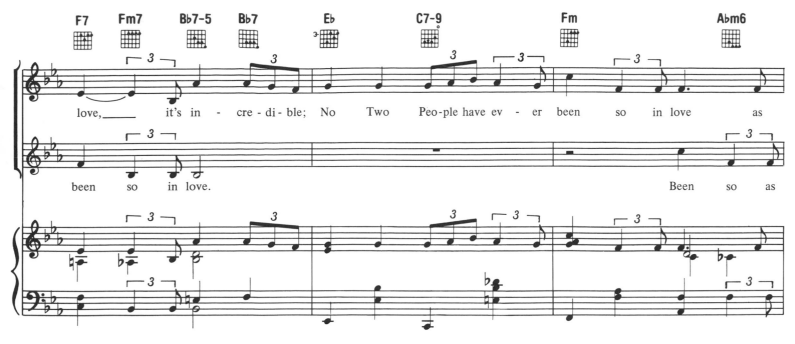

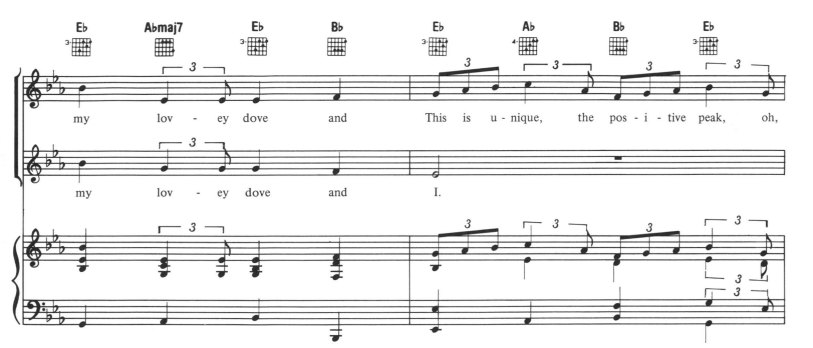

my lov-ey dove and This is the cream, the ve-ry ex-treme, the

my lov-ey dove and I.

sort of a dream you could-n't i-ma-gine at all.

Well an-y-way, No Two Peo-ple have ev - er

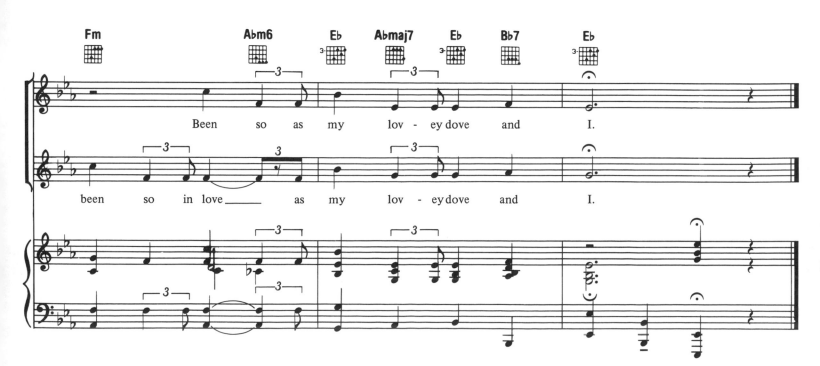

Been so as my lov-ey dove and I.

been so in love ____ as my lov-ey dove and I.

Singin' in the Rain

Music: Nacio Herb Brown
Lyrics: Arthur Freed
Screenplay: Betty Comden & Adolph Green
Produced by: Arthur Freed for MGM
Directors-choreographers: Gene Kelly &
    Stanley Donen
Photography: Harold Rosson (Technicolor)
Cast: Gene Kelly, Donald O'Connor, Debbie Reynolds, Jean
    Hagen, Millard Mitchell, Cyd Charisse, Rita Moreno,
    Jimmy Thompson
Songs: "Singin' in the Rain"; "Fit as a Fiddle" (music: Al
    Hoffman, Al Goodhart); "All I Do Is Dream of You";
    "Make 'Em Laugh"; "I've Got a Feelin' You're Foolin' ";
    "Should I?"; "Beautiful Girl"; "You Were Meant for
    Me"; "Good Morning"; "Would You?"
Released: March 1952; 103 minutes

Gene Kelly's dance to the title song.

Since Arthur Freed had recently produced a movie built around the Gershwin catalogue (*An American in Paris*), and since he himself had begun his career as the lyricist partner of composer Nacio Herb Brown, why not, he reasoned, build a movie around the Freed catalogue? For the project Betty Comden and Adolph Green were chosen to concoct an appropriate tale with no more inspirational guide than the songs Freed and Brown had written for MGM movies during the late 1920s and early 1930s. Because these songs evoked the flavor of the period, the writers came up with a spoofing but affectionate story about the traumatic days when Hollywood abandoned the silent screen in favor of the sound screen. And since the leading male role would be that of a former song-and-dance man who becomes a Hollywood star, the part was eminently suited to Gene Kelly, who was also signed as co-director-choreographer with Stanley Donen. In addition to Comden, Green, Kelly, and Donen, *Singin' in the Rain* also reunited others in the Freed Unit who had worked together on On the Town—associate producer Roger Edens, art director Cedric Gibbons, music director Lennie Hayton, and cameraman Harold Rosson. As in the case of *An American in Paris*, the studio hierarchs wanted a fresh face for the female lead, and they chose the one belonging to Debbie Reynolds.

The story tells of silent screen idol Don Lockwood who accidentally meets Kathy Selden following the premiere of Don's latest swashbuckler, *The Royal Rascal*. Kathy is a struggling young actress who, with the advent of the talkies, gets a job dubbing the speaking voice of a temperamental star, Lina Lamont (Jean Hagen), whose barely understandable squeak would have ended her career. Eventually, the ruse is revealed and Kathy wins both stardom and Don. One curious aspect of *Singin' in the Rain* is that it actually perpetuates the kind of auditory deception that it ridicules. The cultured speaking tones emanating from Miss Hagen's mouth were really her own since Miss Reynolds' Texas twang would have been unsuitable, and even Debbie's singing of "Would You?" had to be dubbed by Betty Noyes.

The picture has a number of standout musical sequences, especially Kelly's splash dance to "Singin' in the Rain," which became his trademark. Donald O'Connor (as Don's sidekick Cosmo Brown) had a funny slapstick number in "Make 'Em Laugh" (though the music and general idea had been snitched from Cole Porter's "Be a Clown"), and there was an exuberant "Good Morning" for Kelly, Reynolds, and O'Connor to perform all over Lockwood's house. The lengthy, self-contained "Broadway Ballet" (which seems to have come out of another film called *Left Field*), finds Kelly playing a young hoofer who wins success on the Great White Way but loses the seductive moll (Cyd Charisse) whom he adores.

Singin' in the Rain is usually on anyone's list of the screen's most favored musicals. Two stage productions were based on the movie. In 1983, a London version with Tommy Steele had a run of two years; in 1985, a Broadway version with Don Correia hung on for ten months.

CBS ST. MGM/UA VC.

Where's Charley?

Music & lyrics: Frank Loesser
Screenplay: John Monks Jr.
Produced by: Gerry Blattner for Warner Bros.
Directed by: David Butler
Choreography: Michael Kidd
Photography: Erwin Hillier (Technicolor)
Cast: Ray Bolger, Allyn McLerie, Robert Shackleton, Mary Germaine, Horace Cooper, Margaretta Scott
Songs: "Once in Love with Amy"; "My Darling, My Darling"; "Make a Miracle"; "Pernambuco"; "Where's Charley?"; "The New Ashmoleon Marching Society and Student Conservatory Band"
Released: July 1952; 97 minutes

In a dream sequence, Ray Bolger and Allyn McLerie dance to the music of "Pernambuco."

For his first Broadway assignment, Hollywood composer-lyricist Frank Loesser was engaged to write the score for the 1948 musical *Where's Charley?*, adapted from Brandon Thomas's durable farce, *Charley's Aunt*. The Thomas play, which premiered in London in 1892, concerns two Oxford undergraduates, Charley Wykeham and Jack Chesney who, in order to entertain two proper young ladies in their rooms, cajole a third student, Lord Fancourt Babberly, to act as chaperon by posing as Charley's aunt from Brazil, "where the nuts come from." (Jack Benny starred in the movie version of *Charley's Aunt* in 1941.) In the musical adaptation, the third character was eliminated and the aunt in drag was played by Charley himself, with the humor resulting from the quick costume changes as Charley runs around trying to play both the aunt and the ardent suitor. Ray Bolger as Charley, Allyn McLerie as his inamorata, and Horace Cooper as Miss McLerie's guardian repeated their stage roles in the screen adaptation, which also retained most of the songs in Loesser's score (including Bolger's showstopping "Once in Love with Amy" and his proposal duet with Miss McLerie, "Make a Miracle"). Part of the film was shot at Oxford.

Once in Love with Amy

FROM WHERE'S CHARLEY?

By FRANK LOESSER

With a Song in My Heart

Screenplay: Lamar Trotti
Produced by: Lamar Trotti for 20th Century-Fox
Directed by: Walter Lang
Choreography: Billy Daniels
Photography: Leon Shamroy (Technicolor)
Cast: Susan Hayward, David Wayne, Thelma Ritter, Rory Calhoun, Una Merkel, Richard Allan, Max Showalter, Leif Erickson, Robert Wagner, Lyle Talbot
Songs: "Blue Moon" (Richard Rodgers-Lorenz Hart); "With a Song in My Heart" (Rodgers-Hart); "Embraceable You" (George Gershwin-Ira Gershwin); "Tea for Two" (Vincent Youmans-Irving Caesar); "It's a Good Day" (Dave Barbour-Peggy Lee); "They're Either Too Young or Too Old" (Arthur Schwartz-Frank Loesser); "I'll Walk Alone" (Jule Styne-Sammy Cahn); "Indiana" (James Hanley-Ballard MacDonald); "Deep in the Heart of Texas" (Don Swander-June Hershey)
Released: February 1952; 117 minutes

Jane Froman (Susan Hayward) entertaining the troops.

A leading radio, nightclub, and recording attraction during the 1930's and 1940's, Jane Froman suffered a crippling accident early in 1943 when she was injured in a plane crash off Lisbon as she was flying to entertain the troops. The story of the singer's battle to recover her health and her gallant professional comeback was the subject of a highly popular if sudsy biography, in which Susan Hayward gave a strong performance and Miss Froman supplied the vocal dubbing on the soundtrack for over 20 songs (including "I'll Walk Alone," which became one of the singer's best-selling records).

Capitol ST.

1952

I'll Walk Alone
FROM WITH A SONG IN MY HEART

Lyric by SAMMY CAHN
Music by JULE STYNE

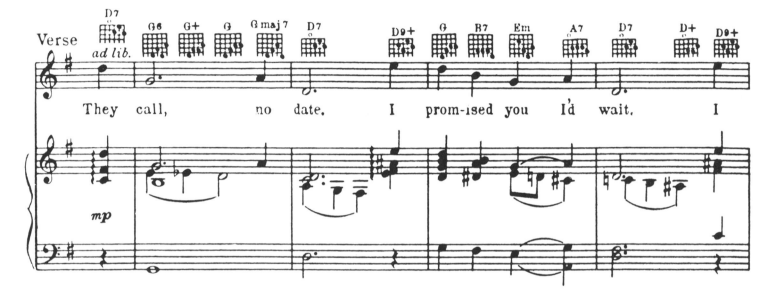

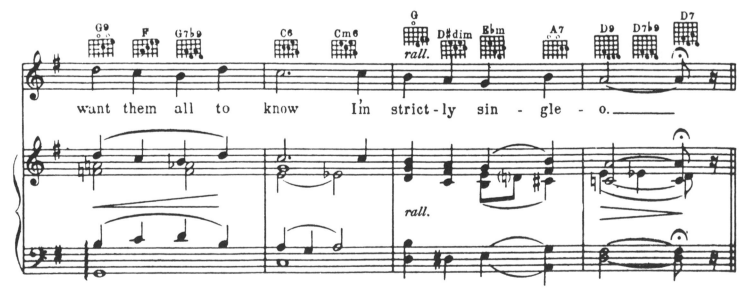

Chorus
Slowly *(in even tempo)*
Guitar tacet

I'LL WALK A - LONE _____ be-cause, to tell you the truth, I'll be

lone - ly. _____ I don't mind be - ing lone - ly _____

_____ When my heart tells me you _____ are lone-ly too. _____ I'LL WALK A -

LONE, _____ they'll ask me why and I'll tell _____ them I'd rath - er; _____

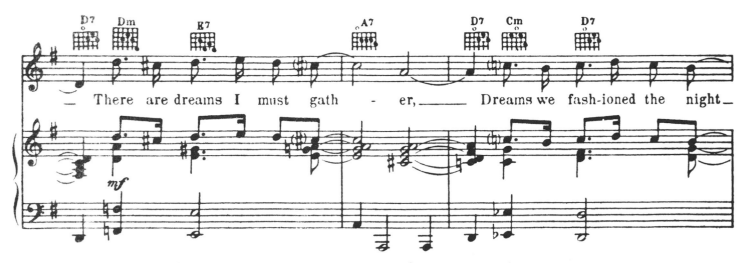

There are dreams I must gath - er,_____ Dreams we fash-ioned the night_

_____ you held me tight. I'll al-ways be near_ you, wher-

ev - er you are,_ Each night_ in ev -'ry prayer. If

you call I'll hear_ you, no mat - ter how far;_ Just close your

eyes ___ and I'll be there. ___ Please walk a - lone ___ and send your

love and your kiss - es to guide me. ___ Till you're walk - ing be - side ___

me, ___ I'LL WALK A - LONE.

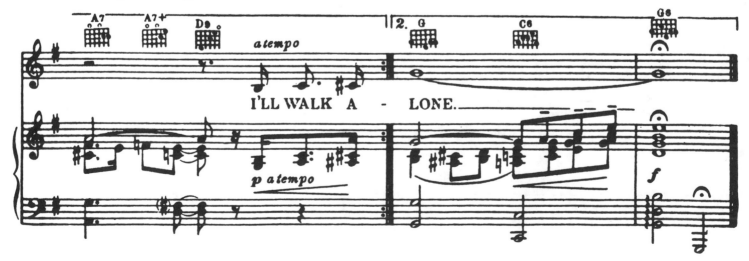

I'LL WALK A - LONE. ___

THE BAND WAGON

Music: Arthur Schwartz
Lyrics: Howard Dietz
Screenplay: Betty Comden & Adolph Green
Produced by: Arthur Freed for MGM
Directed by: Vincente Minnelli
Choreography: Michael Kidd
Photography: Harry Jackson (Technicolor)
Cast: Fred Astaire, Cyd Charisse, Oscar Levant, Nanette Fabray, Jack Buchanan, James Mitchell, Thurston Hall, Ava Gardner, Julie Newmar, Matt Mattox, LeRoy Daniels
Songs: "By Myself"; "UA Shine on Your Shoes"; "That's Entertainment"; "Dancing in the Dark"; "Something to Remember You By"; "High and Low"; "I Love Louisa"; "New Sun in the Sky"; "I Guess I'll Have to Change My Plan"; "Louisiana Hayride"; "Triplets"; "The Girl Hunt" ballet (narration: Alan Jay Lerner)
Released: July 1953; 112 minutes

Fred Astaire, Nanette Fabray, and Jack Buchanan as "Triplets."

With the male lead of *Easter Parade*, the director of *An American in Paris*, and the writers of *Singin' in the Rain*, *The Band Wagon* became the fourth Arthur Freed production to spotlight the catalogue of a major songwriter or team. This time out it was composer Arthur Schwartz and lyricist Howard Dietz (he also doubled as head of MGM's promotion and publicity department), whose songs graced some of Broadway's most sophisticated revues. One of them even supplied the movie with a title. Since the original *Band Wagon* had also starred Fred Astaire (along with his sister Adele), and since Fred would be playing the leading role in the picture, this somehow sparked the idea of a backstage story in which four of the leading characters would be based on actual people. Fred's own career suggested the role of an aging Hollywood song-and-dance man. Comden and Green used themselves as models for two Broadway writers (played by Nanette Fabray and Oscar Levant), and the part of a flamboyant director (played by Jack Buchanan after it had been turned down by Clifton Webb) was a combination of Orson Welles, Jose Ferrer, and director Minnelli himself.

In the story, Tony Hunter, washed up in Hollywood, comes to New York to make a comeback in a musical comedy created by his friends Lily and Lester Marton. The show is to be directed by Broadway's latest genius, Jeffrey Cordova, and the leading lady is to be ballerina Gabrielle Gerard (Cyd Charisse, with India Adams' singing voice). The biggest problem along the show's bumpy road to New York is that Cordova has turned the Martons' lighthearted script into an arty modern version of *Faust*. Disaster! So in true Mickey and Judy style ("Gosh, with all this raw talent around, why can't us kids get together and put on ourselves a show!," was Levant's line), the actors take over the production from Cordova (though he appears in it) and transform it into a Broadway smash. Simple as that.

Among the unforgettable musical numbers are Astaire's rueful "By Myself" in Grand Central Terminal . . . his exuberant "Shine on Your Shoes" with LeRoy Daniels as they scamper around a 42nd Street penny arcade . . . the witty "That's Entertainment" (the only song written for the film) . . . the languid Astaire-Charisse dance to "Dancing in the Dark" performed in Central Park . . . Astaire and Buchanan's debonair song-and-dance to "I Guess I'll Have to Change My Plan" . . .the comic "Triplets" with Astaire, Fabray, and Buchanan on their knees in baby clothes . . . and "The Girl Hunt" ballet (with narration written anonymously by Alan Jay Lerner), a takeoff on Mickey Spillane detective novels featuring Astaire and Charisse.

Four years before *The Band Wagon* reached the screen, Fox had used three songs from the original stage revue in *Dancing in the Dark*, in which William Powell played a washedup Hollywood actor. Earlier in the same year as *The Band Wagon*, Warners' *She's Back on Broadway* also told of a has-been movie star (Virginia Mayo) who attempts a comeback in a stage musical. (She's a hit but the show isn't.)

CBS ST. MGM/UA VC.

1953

That's Entertainment

FROM THE BAND WAGON

Words by HOWARD DIETZ
Music by ARTHUR SCHWARTZ

1. The clown with his pants fall-ing down,
   doubt while the ju-ry is out,

   Or the dance that's a dream of ro-mance,
   Or the thrill when they're read-ing the will,

   Or the scene where the vil-lain is mean;
   Or the chase for the man with the mean face;

   That's en-ter-tain-ment!
   That's en-ter-tain-ment!

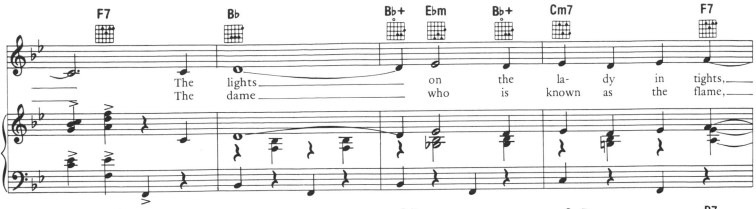

The lights _____ on the la-dy in tights,
The dame _____ who is known as the flame,

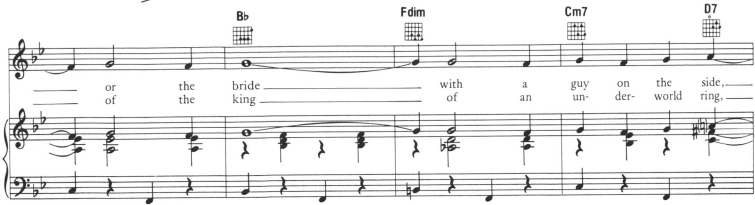

_____ or the bride _____ with a guy on the side,
_____ of the king _____ of an un-der-world ring,

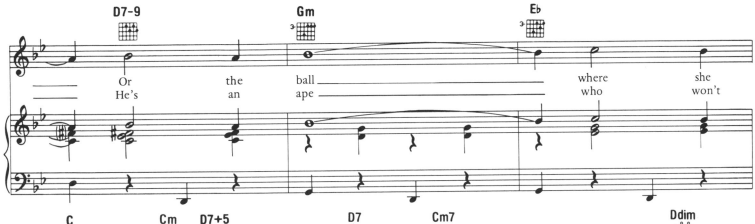

Or the ball _____ where she
He's an ape _____ who won't

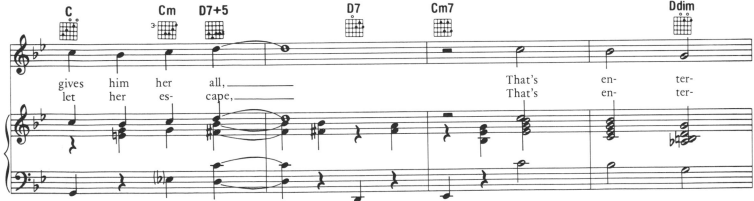

gives him her all, _____ That's en-en-ter-
let her es-cape, _____ That's en-en-ter-

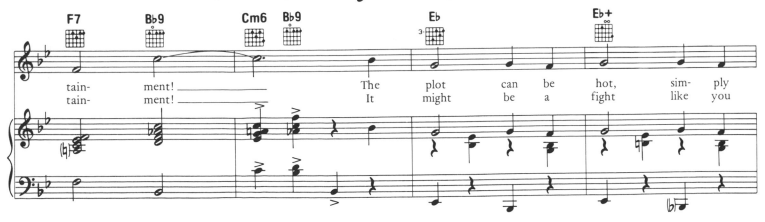

tain-ment! _____ The plot can be hot, sim-ply
tain-ment! _____ It might be a fight like you

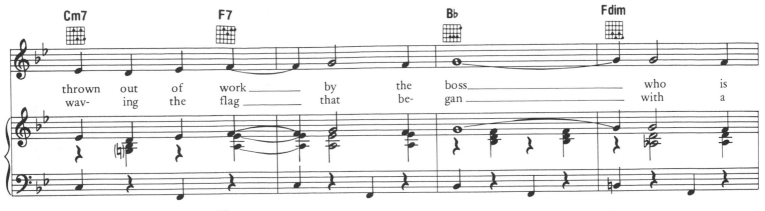

thrown out of work _____ by the boss _____ who is
wav- ing of the flag _____ that be- gan _____ with a

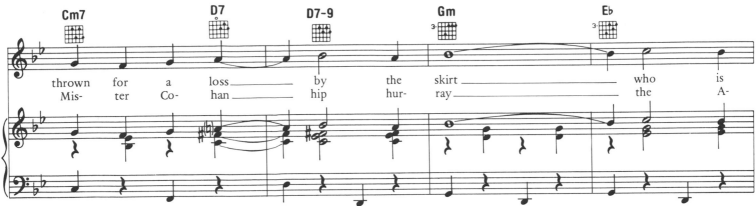

thrown for a loss _____ by the skirt _____ who is
Mis- ter Co- han _____ hip hur- ray _____ the A-

do- ing him dirt; _____ The world is a stage, the
-mer- i- can way; _____ The world is a stage, the

stage is a world of en- en- ter- tain- -
stage is a world of en- ter- tain- -

-ment! The
-ment! _____

Call Me Madam

Music & lyrics: Irving Berlin
Screenplay: Arthur Sheekman
Produced by: Sol C. Siegel for 20th Century-Fox
Directed by: Walter Lang
Choreography: Robert Alton
Photography: Leon Shamroy (Technicolor)
Cast: Ethel Merman, George Sanders, Donald O'Connor, Vera-Ellen, Billy DeWolfe, Helmut Dantine, Walter Slezak, Ludwig Stossel, Charles Dingle, Walter Woolf King, Johnny Downs
Songs: "The Hostess with the Mostes' "; "Can You Use Any Money Today?"; "Marrying for Love"; "It's a Lovely Day Today"; "That International Rag"; "The Ocarina"; "What Chance Have I with Love?"; "The Best Thing for You"; Something to Dance About"; "You're Just in Love"
Released: March 1953; 117 minutes

Ethel Merman belting "Something to Dance About" as she entertains at an embassy party.

O f Ethel Merman's nine Broadway musicals that were turned into movies, only two retained her services—*Anything Goes* in 1936 and *Call Me Madam* 17 years later. A Broadway hit of 1950, *Call Me Madam* had a book by Howard Lindsay and Russel Crouse based on President Harry Truman's surprise choice of wellheeled Washington party-giver Perle Mesta as Ambassador to Luxembourg, and the musical was replete with satirical thrusts at politics, foreign affairs, and the behavior of the comically gauche Americans abroad. The film version—which gave Miss Merman her best screen role—was a close approximation of the show, with virtually all the Irving Berlin songs intact. In the story, when Sally Adams, the hostess with the mostes' on the ball, becomes Ambassador to the mythical Duchy of Lichtenburg, she charms the local gentry with her brash, no-nonsense style. She also finds herself in a romantic foreign entanglement with diplomat Cosmo Constantine (George Sanders in his only screen musical), and helps her young aide, Kenneth Gibson (Donald O'Connor), recognize romantic symptoms in the contrapuntal duet, "You're Just in Love."

DRG ST.

(I Wonder Why?)
You're Just in Love
FROM CALL ME MADAM

Words and Music by
IRVING BERLIN

I hear sing-ing and there's no one there.

I smell blos-soms and the trees are bare.

All day long I seem to walk on air, I won-der

A rub - down with a vel - vet glove. _____

There is noth - ing you can take ___

to re - lieve that pleas - ant ache. ___ You're not sick you're

just in love. _____

CARMEN JONES

Music: Georges Bizet
Lyrics: Oscar Hammerstein II
Screenplay: Harry Kleiner
Producer-director: Otto Preminger for 20th
    Century-Fox
Choreography: Herbert Ross
Photography: Sam Leavitt (Deluxe Color;
    CinemaScope)
Cast: Dorothy Dandridge, Harry Belafonte, Olga
    James, Pearl Bailey, Diahann Carroll, Joe Adams,
    Brock Peters, Carmen DeLavallade
Songs: "Dat's Love"; "You Talk Just Like My Maw";
    "Dere's a Cafe on de Corner"; "Beat Out Dat
    Rhythm on a Drum"; "Stan' Up an' Fight"; "Dis
    Flower"; "My Joe"
Released: October 1954; 105 minutes

Dorothy Dandridge and Harry Belafonte.

French novelist Prosper Mérimée's *Carmen* was brought to the screen ten times as a silent, but it was not until 1948 that the story was filmed in Hollywood with sound (Columbia's *The Loves of Carmen* with Rita Hayworth). The first time, however, that an American studio filmed it with the music of Bizet's 1875 opera was when Fox released *Carmen Jones*, based on Oscar Hammerstein's all-black Broadway version of 1943. The action is now set during World War II mostly in the South and the leading characters are Carmen (Dorothy Dandridge dubbed by Marilyn Horne), a worker in a parachute factory; Joe (Harry Belafonte dubbed by LeVern Hutcherson), an Army corporal who falls in love with the temptress; Cindy Lou (Olga James) the country girl who loves Joe; and Husky Miller (Joe Adams dubbed by Marvin Hayes), a prizefighter who is the cause of Joe's strangling Carmen in a jealous rage. The most recent screen adaptation of Bizet's original opera was in 1984 with Julia Migenes-Johnson.

RCA ST.

1954

Dat's Love
(Habañera)
from Carmen Jones

Lyrics by OSCAR HAMMERSTEIN II
Music by GEORGES BIZET

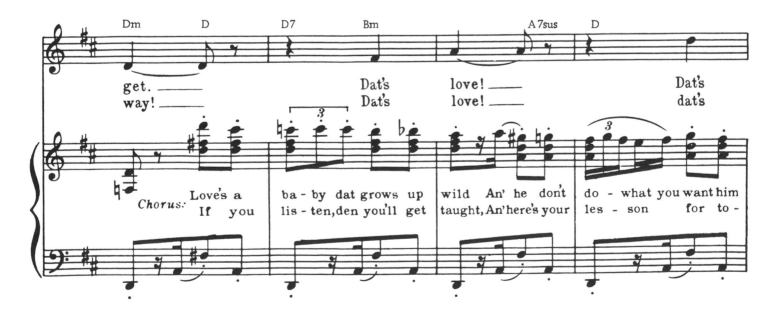

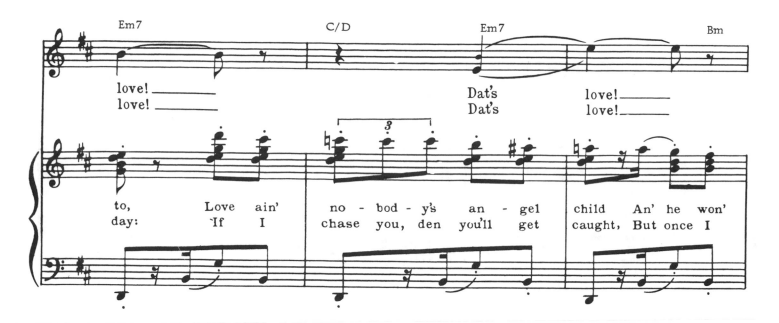

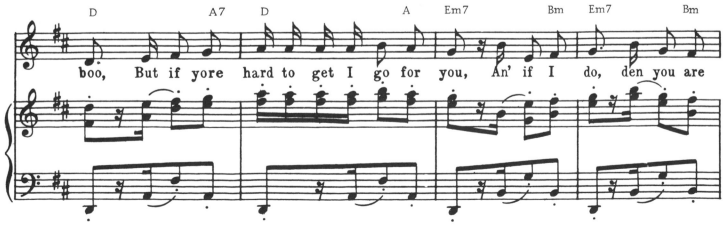

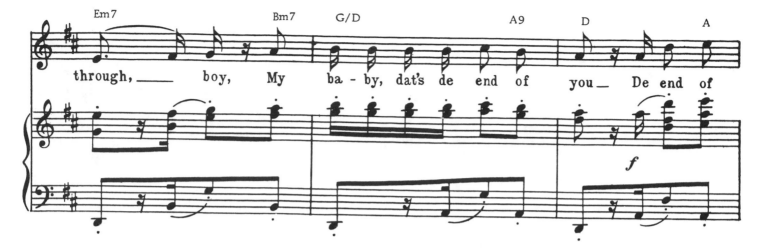

Kiss Me Kate

Music & lyrics: Cole Porter
Screenplay: Dorothy Kingsley
Produced by: Jack Cummings for MGM
Directed by: George Sidney
Choreography: Hermes Pan (Bob Fosse uncredited)
Photography: Charles Rosher (Ansco Color)
Cast: Kathryn Grayson, Howard Keel, Ann Miller, Tommy Rall, Keenan Wynn, James Whitmore, Bobby Van, Bob Fosse, Kurt Kasznar, Ron Randell, Willard Parker, Carol Haney, Jeanne Coyne, Claud Allister, Dave O'Brien
Songs: "So in Love"; "Too Darn Hot"; "Why Can't You Behave?"; "Wunderbar"; "We Open in Venice"; "Tom, Dick or Harry"; "I've Come to Wive It Wealthily in Padua"; "I Hate Men"; "Were Thine That Special Face"; "Where Is the Life That Late I Led?"; "Always True to You (in My Fashion)"; "Brush Up Your Shakespeare"; "From This Moment On"
Released: October 1953; 109 minutes

Howard Keel taming his shrew Kathryn Grayson. Looking on are Bob Fosse, Bobby Van, Ann Miller, and Tommy Rall.

Kiss Me Kate had its genesis in 1935 when Saint Subber, then a stagehand for a Theatre Guild production of Shakespeare's *Taming of the Shrew*, couldn't help but observe that its stars, Alfred Lunt and Lynn Fontanne, battled almost as fiercely offstage as they did in the play. Convinced that this had the makings of a Broadway musical, Subber, who by 1948 had become a producer, took his idea to Cole Porter and playwrights Bella and Samuel Spewack. The result was Porter's most acclaimed work which, in turn, became the most satisfying of all the composer's eight stage musicals adapted to the screen, with virtually the entire score both intact and effectively staged. (Because of censorship, however, "stuck a pig" was changed to "met a bore" in "I've Come to Wive It Wealthily in Padua," and "virgin" became "maiden" in "I Hate Men.")

The movie reunited Kathryn Grayson and Howard Keel for their third and final appearance together (their other films were *Show Boat* and *Lovely to Look At*), though initially producer Jack Cummings had tried to get Laurence Oliver for the male lead. Miss Grayson was seen as Lilli Vanessi, a temperamental actress, and Keel played her exhusband, Fred Graham, an egotistical actor and director, who is anxious to have Lilli costar with him in a musical version of *The Taming of the Shrew* (even Cole Porter, in the person of Ron Randell, shows up to persuade her). Despite misgivings, Lilli agrees, and the story focuses on the show's final rehearsal and out-of-town opening, with the action moving from backstage to onstage. (As in the 1929 film, *On with the Show*, the progress of the play, though seen only in segments, can be easily followed by the movie audience.) Hermes Pan's choreography for Ann Miller's sizzling "Too Darn Hot," and especially for the numbers involving Miss Miller, Tommy Rall, Bobby Van, Bob Fosse, Carol Haney, and Jeanne Coyne, turned the screen version into even more of a dancing show than the original. Fosse, in fact, made his choreographic debut with a segment in the sequence featuring "From This Moment On," a song that had been dropped from another Porter musical, *Out of This World*.

Kiss Me Kate was the only musical filmed in the three dimensional—or 3D—process, an innovation that accounts for the distraction of seeing various items thrown directly at the camera, as well as for the staging of Keel's solo, "Where Is the Life That Late I Led?," on a runway jutting into the on-screen audience. Other movie musicals derived from Shakespearean sources were *The Boys from Syracuse* (1940) from *The Comedy of Errors*; *West Side Story* (1961) from *Romeo and Juliet*; and both *All Night Long* (1961) and *Catch My Soul* (1974) from *Othello*.

CBS ST. MGM/UA VC.

So in Love
FROM KISS ME KATE

Words and Music by
COLE PORTER

know, dar - ling, why, _____ So in

love _____ with you am I, _____ In

love with the night mys - te - ri - ous, _____ The

night when you first were there, _____ In

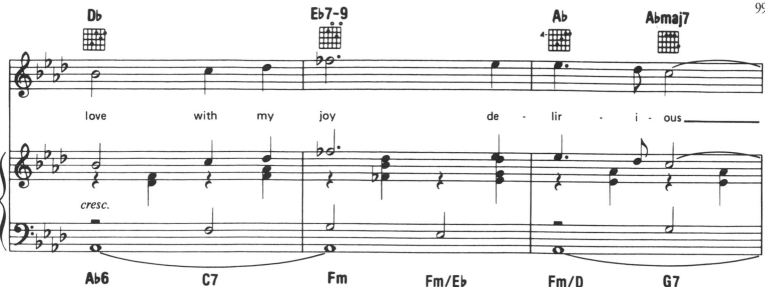

love with my joy de - lir - i - ous _____

cresc.

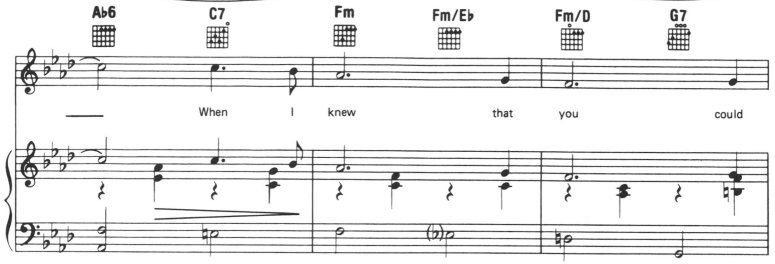

_____ When I knew that you could

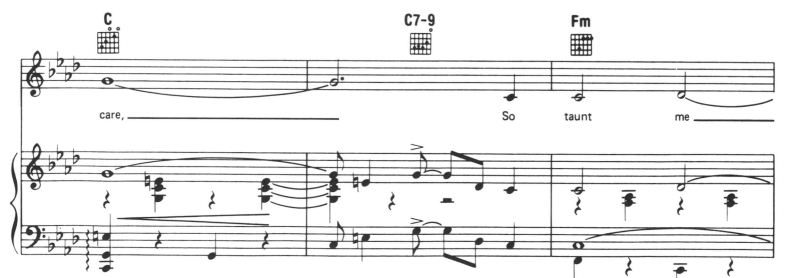

care, _____ So taunt me _____

_____ and hurt me, _____ De -

THE COUNTRY GIRL

Music: Harold Arlen
Lyrics: Ira Gershwin
Screenplay: George Seaton
Produced by: William Perlberg for Paramount
Directed by: George Seaton
Choreography: Robert Alton
Photography: John F. Warren
Cast: Bing Crosby, Grace Kelly, William Holden, Anthony
    Ross, Gene Reynolds, Jacqueline Fontaine
Songs: "The Search Is Through"; "Dissertation on the State
    of Bliss (Love and Learn)"; "It's Mine, It's Yours"; "The
    Land Around Us"
Released: November 1954; 104 minutes

Bing Crosby recording "The Search Is Through."

Based on Clifford Odets' 1950 Broadway play, *The Country Girl* (a rather misleading title) was more of a drama with songs than a musical drama. It also gave Bing Crosby (who had originally turned it down) the most challenging role of his career, and the four Harold Arlen-Ira Gershwin songs seem to have been included to give Crosby confidence rather than to fulfill an essential need in the story. The plot of the film (one of 1955's box office winners) concerns an alcoholic, washed-up singer attempting to make a comeback on the stage in an *Oklahoma!* type musical called *The Land Around Us*, and his relationships with his long-suffering wife (Grace Kelly replaced Jennifer Jones before shooting began), and the show's director (William Holden) who, at first, fails to understand the actor's dependence on his spouse. *The Country Girl* marked Bing Crosby's 45th and penultimate appearance in a Paramount picture.

Decca (Crosby LP). Paramount VC.

Dissertation on the State of Bliss
(Love and Learn)
from the Motion Picture THE COUNTRY GIRL

Lyric by IRA GERSHWIN
Music by HAROLD ARLEN

THE GLENN MILLER STORY

Screenplay: Valentine Davies & Oscar Brodney
Produced by: Aaron Rosenberg for Universal
Directed by: Anthony Mann
Photography: William Daniels (Technicolor)
Cast: James Stewart, June Allyson, Harry Morgan, Charles Drake, George Tobias, Frances Langford, Louis Armstrong, Gene Krupa, Ben Pollack, Barton MacLane, Sig Rumann, Kathleen Lockhart
Songs: "Basin Street Blues" (Spencer Williams); "Over the Rainbow" (Harold Arlen-E. Y. Harburg); "I Know Why" (Harry Warren-Mack Gordon); "String of Pearls" (Jerry Gray-Eddie DeLange); "Pennsylvania 6-5000" (Gray-Carl Sigman); "Tuxedo Junction" (Erskine Hawkins, William Johnson, Julian Dash-Buddy Feyne); "Chattanooga Choo-Choo" (Warren-Gordon)
Released: January 1954; 116 minutes

James Stewart as Glenn Miller.

A highly sentimentalized biography of one of the major figures of the big-band era, *The Glenn Miller Story* was Hollywood's most popular movie about the life of an orchestra leader (it had the eighth highest theatre rental fees of any musical released during the 1950's). James Stewart gave a sensitive performance in the title role (Joe Yukl dubbed his trombone playing), which helped overcome some of the excesses in the cliché-filled script dealing with Miller's domestic life (June Allyson played the understanding little woman) and his messianic search for "my own sound." Miller himself appeared in *Sun Valley Serenade* (1941) and *Orchestra Wives* (1942). Other screen biographies of bandleaders of the period were *The Fabulous Dorseys* (Jimmy and Tommy played themselves), *The Benny Goodman Story* (Steve Allen), *The Eddy Duchin Story* (Tyrone Power), and *The Gene Krupa Story* (Sal Mineo).

MCA ST. MCA VC.

A String of Pearls

FROM THE GLENN MILLER STORY

Words by EDDIE DeLANGE
Music by JERRY GRAY

Moderately Bright

Ba - by___ Here's ___ a five and dime, Ba - by___ Now's___
Ba - by___ {You} I ___ made quite a start, found the___ way___

___ a - bout the time For A ___ String ___ Of Pearls a - la
___ right to {my}{your} heart With A ___ String ___ Of Pearls a - la

Wool - worth. Ev - 'ry___ pearl's ___ a star a - bove
Wool - worth. Wait 'til the ___ stars peek-a - boo,

8va bassa- -

Seven Brides for Seven Brothers

Music: Gene de Paul
Lyrics: Johnny Mercer
Screenplay: Frances Goodrich, Albert Hackett, Dorothy Kingsley
Produced by: Jack Cummings for MGM
Directed by: Stanley Donen
Choreography: Michael Kidd
Photography: George Folsey (Ansco Color; CinemaScope)
Cast: Jane Powell, Howard Keel, Jeff Richards, Russ Tamblyn, Tommy Rall, Marc Platt, Matt Mattox, Jacques d'Amboise, Julie Newmar, Virginia Gibson, Kelly Brown
Songs: "Bless Your Beautiful Hide"; "Wonderful, Wonderful Day"; "When You're in Love"; "Goin' Co'tin' "; "Lonesome Polecat"; "Sobbin' Women"; "Spring, Spring, Spring"
Released: June 1954; 103 minutes

The barn - raising sequence.

Based on Stephen Vincent Benet's story, "The Sobbin' Women"—which had been based on Plutarch's "Rape of the Sabine Women"—*Seven Brides for Seven Brothers* switched the locale from the Tennessee Valley to the Oregon backwoods in 1850 and turned the tale into a thick slice of robust Americana. Farmer Adam Pontipee (Howard Keel) goes to town looking for a wife and quickly finds a cook named Milly (Jane Powell) to marry him. Milly soon discovers, much to her horror, that Adam shares his isolated farmhouse with six surly, unwashed younger brothers. She tries teaching them social graces ("Goin' Co'tin' "), but the young men are so romantically frustrated that they take direct action by kidnapping six young women from town. Because an avalanche blocks the mountain pass to the farm, the brothers cannot be apprehended until spring. By then, however, the captives have grown to love their honorably intentioned captors (the girls sleep in the farmhouse, the boys in the barn), and—as the title indicates—the film ends in matrimony for all.

What makes the movie memorable is its ambitious use of dance and the fact that all six younger Pontipees are played by expert dancers. Choreographer Michael Kidd gave them two outstanding sequences: the vaulting, somersaulting barn-raising number which builds to a free-for-all when the brothers square off against the young men from town, and the "Lonesome Polecat" scene in the snow in which the Pontipee boys reveal their misery at being without female companionship. In 1982, a stage version starring Debbie Boone had a brief run on Broadway.

MCA ST. MGM/UA VC.

1954

A STAR IS BORN

Music: Harold Arlen, etc.
Lyrics: Ira Gershwin, etc.
Screenplay: Moss Hart
Produced by: Sidney Luft for
Warner Bros.
Directed by: George Cukor
Choreography: Richard Barstow
Photography: Sam Leavitt
(Technicolor; CinemaScope)
Cast: Judy Garland, James Mason,
Jack Carson, Charles Bickford,
Tommy Noonan, Lucy Marlow,
Grady Sutton, Laurindo Almeida,
Amanda Blake, Irving Bacon,
Louis Jean Heydt, Chick Chandler,
Rex Evans, Mae Marsh
Songs: "Gotta Have Me Go with You"; "The Man That Got Away";
"Born in a Trunk" (Roger Edens-Leonard Gershe); "Swanee"
(George Gershwin-Irving Caesar); "It's a New World"; "Here's What
I'm Here For"; "Someone at Last"; "Lose That Long Face"
Released: September 1954; 154 minutes

Judy Garland singing "The Man That Got Away."

Ever since appearing in a radio adaptation of *A Star Is Born* in 1942, Judy Garland had tried to interest MGM in the property. It was not, however, until the studio cancelled her contract nine years later that she again thought of the venerable Hollywood saga. Judy's then husband, Sidney Luft, made a deal with Warner Bros., and lined up director George Cukor (for his first musical), writer Moss Hart, and songwriters Harold Arlen and Ira Gershwin. Cary Grant, Ray Milland, Humphrey Bogart, Marlon Brando, and Laurence Olivier were sought for the male lead which eventually went to James Mason. The picture cost over $6 million and took ten months to make. Delays were caused by the decision, after eight days' shooting, to film it in CinemaScope, plus Judy's frequent absences from the set, and assorted firings and hirings. After the filming had been completed, the rousing but superfluous 15 minute mini-musical, "Born in a Trunk," was added. This made the running time more than three hours, which—over Cukor's objections—forced the removal of some crucial scenes and the elimination of two songs, "Here's What I'm Here For" and "Lose That Long Face." In 1983, however, most of the deleted sequences were restored and the film was re-released in a version running 170 minutes.

The basic story first showed up in 1932 in David O. Selznick's *What Price Hollywood*, also directed by Cukor, with Constance Bennett as a waitress who becomes a star and Lowell Sherman as her mentor, a heavy-drinking director who hits the skids and shoots himself to death. The second version, in 1937—now called *A Star Is Born*—was again produced by Selznick. This time the movie played up the romantic

relationship by having the rising star (Janet Gaynor) fall in love with and marry a boozy falling star (Fredric March) who ends his life by drowning in the Pacific. (The character was partly based on silent film actor John Bowers, an alcoholic who committed suicide in the same way.)

The emotion-draining musical version of 1954 concerns Esther Blodgett (Garland), a band singer in Hollywood, who, while appearing in a benefit show, encounters a soused movie star, Norman Maine (Mason), when he staggers onstage to join her act. Once he hears Esther sing "The Man That Got Away" in a deserted nightclub, Maine becomes convinced that she could become a great movie actress. With his help, Esther (now known as Vicki Lester) wins a starring role, becomes a sensation, and the couple marries. But Norman's career goes steadily downhill until, to keep from being a burden, the actor walks out of his Malibu beach house and drowns himself. Months later, Esther bravely appears at a benefit show at the Shrine Auditorium. Greeted by an ovation, she steps to the microphone, fights back the tears, and utters the imperishable line, "Hello, everybody. This is . . . Mrs. Norman Maine." (One curious aspect of the film is that the character of the alcoholic, self-destructive actor was more closely identified with Judy Garland's own life than the part she herself played.)

CSP ST. Warner VC.

The Man that Got Away

FROM THE MOTION PICTURE A STAR IS BORN

Lyric by IRA GERSHWIN
Music by HAROLD ARLEN

The night is bit-ter, the stars have lost their glit-ter, the winds grow cold-er, and sud-den-ly you're old-er, and all be-cause of the {man/gal} that got a-way. No more {his/her} eag-er call; the

There's No Business Like Show Business

Music & lyrics: Irving Berlin
Screenplay: Henry & Phoebe Ephron
Produced by: Sol C. Siegel for 20th Century-Fox
Directed by: Walter Lang
Choreography: Robert Alton, Jack Cole
Photography: Leon Shamroy (DeLuxe Color; CinemaScope)
Cast: Ethel Merman, Donald O'Connor, Marilyn Monroe, Dan Dailey, Johnnie Ray, Mitzi Gaynor, Hugh O'Brian, Frank McHugh, Lee Patrick, Chick Chandler, Lyle Talbot
Songs: "When the Midnight Choo-Choo Leaves for Alabam' "; "Play a Simple Melody"; "After You Get What You Want You Don't Want It"; "A Man Chases a Girl (Until She Catches Him)"; "You'd Be Surprised"; "Heat Wave"; "Alexander's Ragtime Band"
Released: December 1954; 117 minutes

Ethel Merman, Dan Dailey in their vaudeville number, "When the Midnight Choo - Choo Leaves for Alabam'."

Because of Ethel Merman's success in *Call Me Madam*, Fox's Darryl Zanuck signed her to appear in a second film with songs by Irving Berlin (including the title number, which Miss Merman had introduced in *Annie Get Your Gun*). The new picture also had the same producer, director, choreographer (Robert Alton), art directors (Lyle Wheeler, John DeCuir), music director (Alfred Newman), choral director (Ken Darby), and editor (Robert Simpson), and the stellar cast included Dan Dailey (as Miss Merman's husband and vaudeville partner), Donald O'Connor, Mitzi Gaynor, and Johnnie Ray (as their dancing and singing children), and, as O'Connor's love interest, Marilyn Monroe (who does a sexy "Heat Wave"). Berlin's score, the last one he worked on for the movies, consisted of 12 songs from the trunk and two new ones.

Decca ST. CBS/Fox VC.

1954

Heat Wave

FROM THERE'S NO BUSINESS LIKE SHOW BUSINESS

Words and Music by
IRVING BERLIN

A heat wave blew right in-to town __ last week.

She came from the Is-land of Mar-tin-ique. __

The can - can she danc - es will make you fry. _____

The can - can is real - ly the rea - son why. _____

We're hav - ing a heat _ wave, _____

a trop - i - cal heat _ wave. _____ The

WHITE CHRISTMAS

Music & lyrics: Irving Berlin
Screenplay: Norman Krasna, Norman Panama, Melvin Frank
Produced by: Robert Dolan for Paramount
Directed by: Michael Curtiz
Choreography: Robert Alton
Photography: Loyal Griggs (Technicolor; VistaVision)
Cast: Bing Crosby, Danny Kaye, Rosemary Clooney, Vera-Ellen, Dean Jagger, Grady Sutton, Sig Rumann, Barrie Chase, George Chakiris
Songs: "White Christmas"; "The Old Man"; "Blue Skies"; "Sisters"; "The Best Things Happen While You're Dancing"; "Snow"; "Mandy"; "Count Your Blessings Instead of Sheep"; "Love, You Didn't Do Right by Me"
Released: August 1954; 120 minutes

Rosemary Clooney, Danny Kaye, Bing Crosby, Vera - Ellen and kids.

Planned as the third Bing Crosby-Fred Astaire-lrving Berlin musical, *White Christmas* suffered the loss of Astaire when Fred took sick and had to be replaced by Donald O'Connor. Then O'Connor took sick and had to be replaced by Danny Kaye. None of the changes affected the box office: grossing $12 million in theatre rentals, the movie held the No. 1 position as the top money-making picture of 1954, and it also ranks fifth among the highest rental musicals of the decade. The story easily shows its *Holiday Inn-Blue Skies* roots, with Crosby and Kaye as successful Broadway partners who become romantically involved with sisters Rosemary Clooney and Vera-Ellen. On vacation in Vermont, they stay at a ski resort owned by Bing and Danny's former Army General (Dean Jagger) where they are the only guests because there's no snow. The boys help out the General by staging their Broadway-bound revue at the resort and Crosby makes a television appeal to his army buddies to show up on Christmas Eve. They do, it snows, and everyone sings "White Christmas."

MCA ST. Paramount VC.

Sisters
From White Christmas

Words and Music by
IRVING BERLIN

Daddy Long Legs

Music & lyrics: Johnny Mercer
Screenplay: Phoebe & Henry Ephron
Produced by: Samuel G. Engel for 20th Century-Fox
Directed by: Jean Negulesco
Choreography: David Robel, Roland Petit (Fred Astaire uncredited)
Photography: Leon Shamroy (DeLuxe Color; CinemaScope)
Cast: Fred Astaire, Leslie Caron, Terry Moore, Thelma Ritter, Fred Clark, Ralph Dumke, Larry Keating, Ray Anthony Orch.
Songs: "History of the Beat"; "Dream"; "Sluefoot"; "Something's Gotta Give"
Released: May 1955; 126 minutes

Fred Astaire and Leslie Caron dancing to "Something's Gotta Give" on a Manhattan terrace.

First filmed in 1919 (with Mary Pickford and Mahlon Hamilton), then in 1931 (with Janet Gaynor and Warner Baxter), the Jean Webster novel gave Fred Astaire, in his mid-fifties, the chance to play an unconventional character of his own age who, though not a performer, likes nothing better than singing, dancing, and playing the drums. In the tale, a wealthy businessman, to forestall gossip about his motive, becomes the anonymous sponsor of an orphan girl's education. They meet without the girl knowing who he is, they fall in love, and eventually the truth comes out. The musical version alters the basic story slightly by making the girl a French orphan (because Darryl Zanuck cast Leslie Caron in the part) who is sent to school in the United States. (The title refers to the fact that initially the only sight the girl has of her benefactor is his distorted, spidery shadow which prompts her to dub him her "Daddy Long Legs"—or in this case, "Papa Faucheux.") Johnny Mercer's score yielded "Something's Gotta Give" (an amatory application of the physical law about irresistible forces and immovable objects), and there were two extended dance sequences—both performed to the song "Dream" in which Miss Caron fantasizes about her middle-aged guardian angel.

1955

Something's Gotta Give

FROM DADDY LONG LEGS

Words and Music by
JOHNNY MERCER

Rather slowly

When an ___ ir - re - sist - i - ble force such as you ___ meets an ___ old ___ im - mov - a - ble ob - ject like me, ___

GUYS AND DOLLS

Music & lyrics: Frank Loesser
Screenplay: Joseph L. Mankiewicz
Produced by: Samuel Goldwyn (released by MGM)
Directed by: Joseph L. Mankiewicz
Choreography: Michael Kidd
Photography: Harry Stradling (Eastman Color; CinemaScope)
Cast: Marlon Brando, Jean Simmons, Frank Sinatra, Vivian Blaine, Robert Keith, Stubby Kaye, B.S. Pully, Johnny Silver, Sheldon Leonard, Danny Dayton, George E. Stone, Regis Toomey, Kathryn Givney, Veda Ann Borg
Songs: "Fugue for Tinhorns"; "The Oldest Established", "I'll Know", "Pet Me, Poppa", "Adelaide's Lament'; "Guys and Dolls", "Adelaide" "A Woman in Love"; "If I Were a Bell", "Take Back Your Mink" "Luck Be a Lady"; "Sue Me"; "Sit Down, You're Rockin' the Boat"
Released: November 1955; 150 minutes

"Luck Be a Lady" sings Marlon Brando as he throws the dice. Among the onlookers: B.S. Pully, Sheldon Leonard, Johnny Silver, Frank Sinatra, and Stubby Kaye.

Samuel Goldwyn paid a record $1 million (plus 10% of the world gross) to secure the screen rights to the classic 1950 stage musical about Broadway's gambling tinhorns (based on Damon Runyon's "The Idyll of Miss Sarah Brown"), then spent $5.5 million of his own money to produce the film. To protect his investment, Goldwyn signed Vivian Blaine to recreate her role of Miss Adelaide, the leading attraction at the Hot Box nightclub, rounded up three of the show's flashiest performers, Stubby Kaye (to repeat his memorable "Sit Down, You're Rockin' the Boat"), B.S. Pully and Johnny Silver, and chose the original stage choreographer, Michael Kidd, for the dances. He also retained 11 of Frank Loesser's 16 songs, to which the composer added "Pet Me, Poppa" (replacing "A Bushel and a Peck"), the Latin-flavored "A Woman in Love" (replacing "I've Never Been in Love Before"), and "Adelaide."

The producer, however, was not above doing some gambling of his own by casting the principal roles with actors who had never before sung in front of a camera—Marlon Brando as the highrolling Sky Masterson (after the more logical first choice, Gene Kelly, had been unable to secure a loanout from MGM) and Jean Simmons as the straitlaced Miss Sarah Brown, the Save-a-Soul Mission doll who falls in love with the smooth-talking guy. Frank Sinatra was tapped for the uncharacteristic role of Nathan Detroit, the harried proprietor of "the oldest established permanent floating crap game in New York," though he was convinced he would have been more suited to the part of Sky Masterson. Goldwyn took another gamble by entrusting both the film's direction and adaptation (of Abe Burrows' libretto) to Joseph Mankiewicz, who had had no previous experience working on a musical. But the most daring decision of all was to try to avoid the realism inherent in movies by having Broadway designer Oliver Smith create purposely stylized, two-dimensional sets that emphasized the artificiality of the hard-shelled but soft-centered characters who populate the very special world of Damon Runyon. Risky or not, it all paid off commercially—if not artistically—when *Guys and Dolls* topped the list as the biggest money-maker of 1956.

The first movie with songs that was derived from a Damon Runyon story was *Little Miss Marker*, a Shirley Temple vehicle of 1934, which was remade three times. After *Guys and Dolls* opened on Broadway, its success spawned three other Runyon-derived releases with songs—*The Lemon Drop Kid* in 1951 (Bob Hope), *Bloodhounds of Broadway* in 1952 (Mitzi Gaynor), and *Money from Home* in 1953 (Dean Martin and Jerry Lewis). In 1989, *Bloodhounds of Broadway* was remade with Madonna in a leading role.

Motion Pic. Tracks ST. CBS/Fox VC.

1955

Luck Be a Lady
FROM GUYS AND DOLLS

By FRANK LOESSER

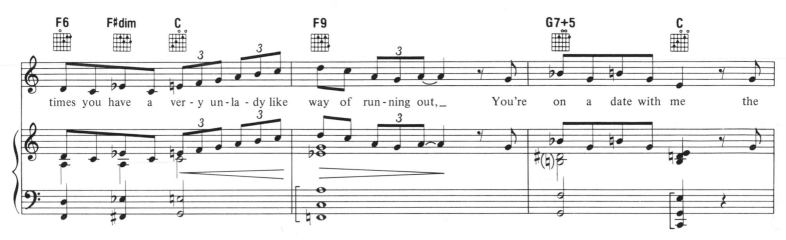

They call you La - dy Luck but there is room for doubt At

times you have a ver - y un - la - dy like way of run - ning out,_ You're on a date with me the

pick - ings have been lush And yet be - fore this eve - ning is ov - er you might give me the brush._ You

might for - get your man - ners, you might re - fuse to stay, And so the best that I can do is

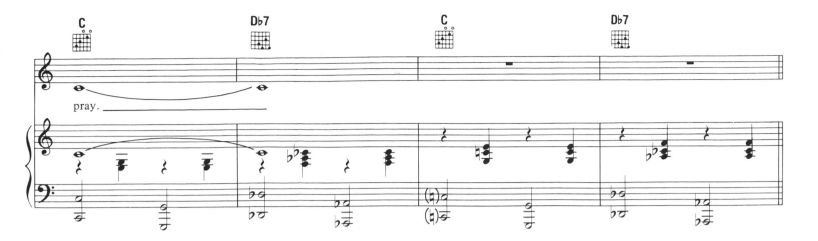

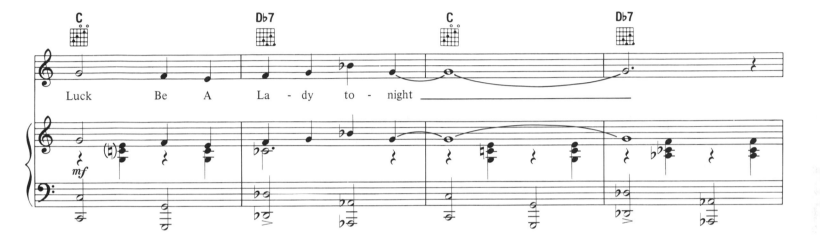

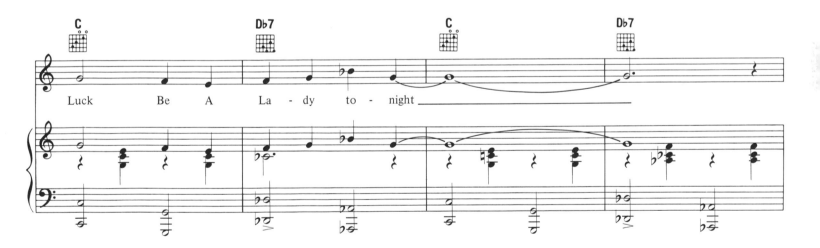

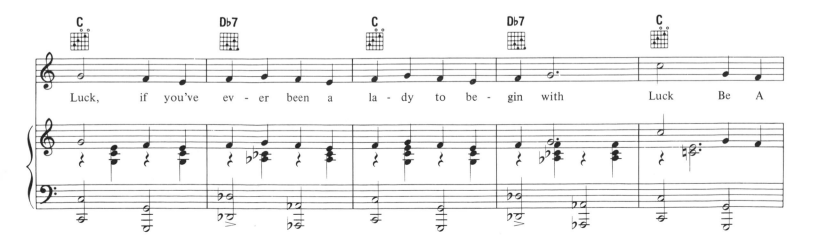

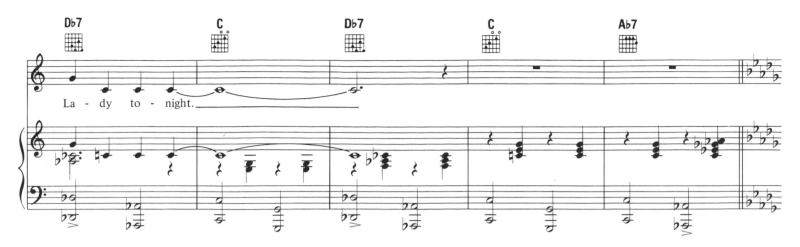

La - dy to - night._____

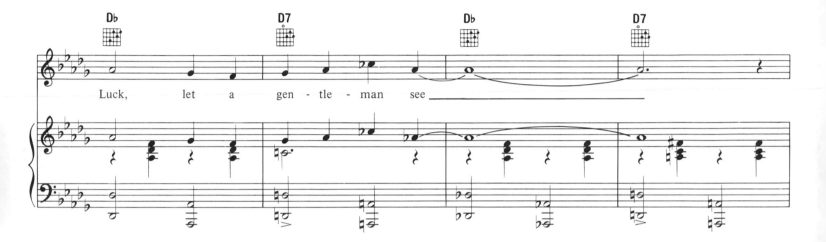

Luck, let a gen - tle - man see _____

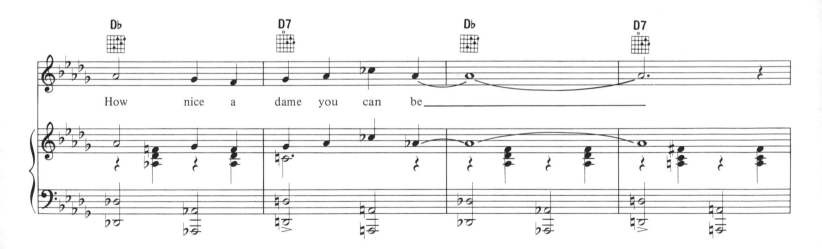

How nice a dame you can be _____

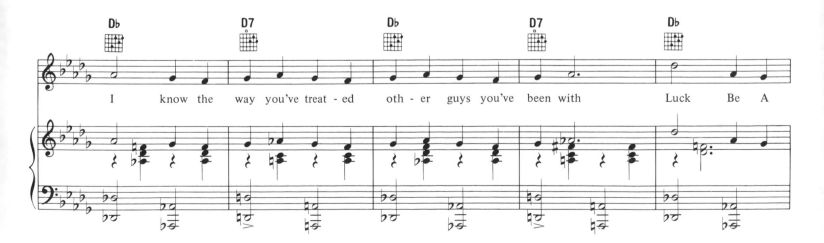

I know the way you've treat - ed oth - er guys you've been with Luck Be A

KISMET

Music: Robert Wright & George Forrest, based on Alexander Borodin
Lyrics: Robert Wright & George Forrest
Screenplay: Charles Lederer & Luther Davis
Produced by: Arthur Freed for MGM
Directed by: Vincente Minnelli (Stanley Donen uncredited)
Choreography: Jack Cole
Photography: Joseph Ruttenberg (Eastman Color; CinemaScope)
Cast: Howard Keel, Ann Blyth, Vic Damone, Dolores Gray, Monty Woolley, Sebastian Cabot, Jay C. Flippen, Aaron Spelling
Songs: "Fate"; "Not Since Nineveh"; "Baubles, Bangles, and Beads"; "Stranger in Paradise"; "Bored"; "Night of My Nights"; "The Olive Tree"; "And This Is My Beloved"; "Sands of Time"
Released: December 1955; 113 minutes

Howard Keel and Ann Blyth.

Set in and around ancient Baghdad, *Kismet* relates the adventures of a public poet (Howard Keel) who in a 24-hour period from dawn to dawn assumes the identity of a beggar named Hajj, then manages to win a fortune, escape from the police, drown the wicked Wazir of Police (Sebastian Cabot), gain appointment to a high government post, and make off with the Wazir's voluptuous wife (Dolores Gray). Oh, yes, he also sees his daughter (Ann Blyth) marry the handsome Caliph (Vic Damone). The movie was an opulent adaptation (written by the show's librettists, Charles Lederer and Luther Davis) of the successful 1953 stage production starring Alfred Drake, for which Robert Wright and George Forrest had created songs based on themes by Alexander Borodin, e.g., "Stranger in Paradise" from the Polovetsian Dances, and both "And This Is My Beloved" and "Baubles, Bangles and Beads" from the D-major String quartet. *Kismet* dates back to a 1911 play by Edward Knoblock, written as a vehicle for Otis Skinner, who appeared in the 1920 and 1930 screen versions (the latter with Loretta Young). A third nonmusical treatment in 1944 costarred Ronald Colman and Marlene Dietrich.

CBS ST. MGM/UA VC.

Stranger in Paradise

FROM KISMET

Words and Music by ROBERT WRIGHT
and GEORGE FORREST
(Music Based on THEMES OF A. BORODIN)

Take my hand,_____ I'm a strang- er in par- a- dise, All lost in a

won- der- land,_____ A strang- er in par- a- dise. If I stand

star- ry- eyed,_____ That's a dan- ger in par- a- dise For mor- tals who

LADY AND THE TRAMP

Music & lyrics: Sonny Burke & Peggy Lee
Screenplay: Erdman Penner, Joe Rinaldi, Ralph
    Wright, Donald Da Gradi
Produced by: Walt Disney (released by
    Buena Vista)
Directed by: Hamilton Luske, Clyde Geronimi,
    Wildred Jackson (Technicolor; Cinema-Scope)
Voices: Peggy Lee, Barbara Luddy, Larry Roberts,
    Bill Thompson, Bill Baucon, Stan Freberg, Verna
    Felton, Alan Reed, George Givot
Songs: "He's a Tramp"; "La La Lu"; "Siamese Cat
    Song"; "Peace on Earth"; "Bella Notte"
Released: April 1955; 75 minutes

Lady, Tramp and pups.

Based on an original story by Ward Greene, *Lady and the Tramp* was put together by a creative staff including over 150 animators and artists. It was also the first Walt Disney cartoon feature in two years and the first in CinemaScope. The film's locale is a New England town in 1910, and the story concerns Lady, a pampered cocker spaniel owned by the improbably named Darling and Jim Dear, who becomes friendly with Tramp, a raffish street mutt from the wrong side of town. When the Dears have a child, Lady not only feels rejected but must also cope with the antagonism of her owners' Aunt Sarah. Lady and Tramp save the life of the newborn baby from a ferocious rat, an act of heroism that is misunderstood by Sarah, who has the dog catcher take Tramp away. The mutt is rescued with the help of Jock, a Scottish terrier, and Trusty, a basset hound, and when last seen Lady and Tramp are the proud parents of a litter of four.

Decca (Lee LP). Disney VC.

1955

Bella Notte
from Walt Disney's Lady and the Tramp

Words and Music by PEGGY LEE
and SONNY BURKE

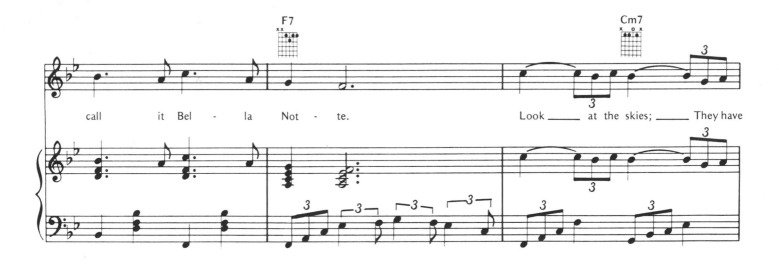

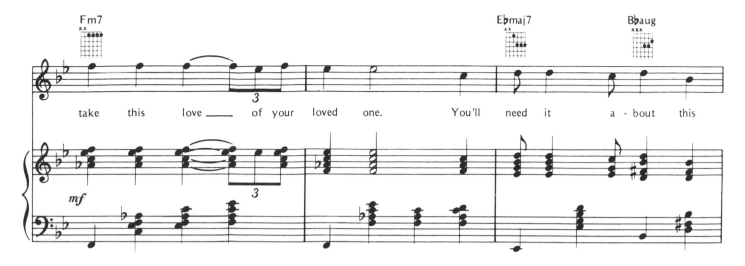

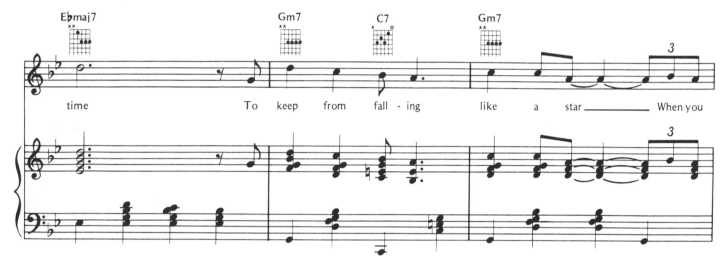

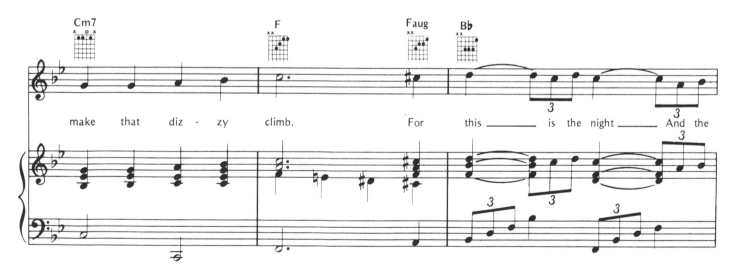

Oklahoma!

Music: Richard Rodgers
Lyrics: Oscar Hammerstein II
Screenplay: Sonya Levien & William Ludwig
Produced by: Arthur Hornblow Jr. for Magna
Directed by: Fred Zinnemann
Choreography: Agnes de Mille
Photography: Robert Surtees (Eastman Color; Todd-AO)
Cast: Gordon MacRae, Gloria Grahame, Shirley Jones, Charlotte Greenwood, Eddie Albert, Gene Nelson, James Whitmore, Rod Steiger, Jay C. Flippen, Marc Platt, James Mitchell, Bambi Linn, Kelly Brown, Barbara Lawrence
Songs: "Oh, What a Beautiful Mornin' "; "The Surrey with the Fringe on Top"; "Kansas City"; "I Cain't Say No"; "Many a New Day"; "People Will Say We're in Love"; "Pore Jud"; "Out of My Dreams"; "The Farmer and the Cowman"; "All er Nothin' "; "Oklahoma"
Released: October 1955; 145 minutes

Shirley Jones and Gordon MacRae.

An acknowledged Broadway landmark, *Oklahoma!*, which opened in 1943, was a major step in the evolution of a more closely integrated form of musical theatre. It also launched the partnership of Richard Rodgers and Oscar Hammerstein II, who based their work on a 1931 play by Lynn Riggs, *Green Grow the Lilacs*. Set in Oklahoma Territory shortly after the turn of the century, the simple tale tells of ranchhand Curly McLain who loves Laurey Williams and hopes to escort her—in his imaginary surrey with the fringe on top—to a box social. Matters are complicated, however, when in a fit of spite Laurey accepts the invitation of the menacing farmhand, Jud Fry. Eventually, Laurey and Curly are married and celebrate the event by leading everyone in singing the praises of their brand new state. The merry-making is interrupted when Jud picks a fight with Curly and accidentally stabs himself to death. Curly is exonerated on the spot and he and Laurey drive off for their honeymoon in a real surrey with the fringe on top. A contrasting comic plot involves Ado Annie Carnes, the girl who cain't say no, and her two admirers, rancher Will Parker and itinerant Persian peddler Ali Hakim. The stage *Oklahoma!* prompted at least two Western movie musicals, *Can't Help Singing* and *The Harvey Girls*, which were released before the show was brought to the screen.

Unwilling to jeopardize *Oklahoma!'s* success on the stage, Rodgers and Hammerstein waited until after the record-breaking Broadway run and the national tour had ended before entering into an agreement with a new company, Magna Theatre Corporation, to produce *Oklahoma!* as the first film released in a new wide-screen process known as Todd-AO (though a year after its initial showing, the film was re-released by 20th Century-Fox in CinemaScope).

Of the original Broadway cast, only dancers Bambi Linn and Marc Platt were in the film version, though the movie did retain the services of choreographer Agnes de Mille, music director Jay Blackton, and orchestrator Robert Russell Bennett. Two songs, "It's a Scandal! It's a Outrage!" and "Lonely Room" were dropped from the original score.

Fred Zinnemann, who had never before worked on a musical, was chosen to direct. Before the major roles were assigned to Gordon MacRae, Shirley Jones (in her first film), and Rod Steiger, Paul Newman and James Dean had been tested for Curly, Joanne Woodward for Laurey, and Eli Wallach for Jud. Charlotte Greenwood, who had been sought for the role of Laurey's aunt in the original production, played the part in the screen version. Though the interiors were filmed in Culver City, most of the exterior locations were shot near Nogales, Arizona, because its terrain was considered closer to turn-of-the-century Oklahoma than the state being celebrated.

Capitol ST. CBS/Fox VC.

People Will Say We're in Love

FROM OKLAHOMA!

Lyrics by OSCAR HAMMERSTEIN II
Music by RICHARD RODGERS

1. Why do they think up stor-ies that link my name with yours?
2. Some peo-ple claim that you are to blame as much as I

Why do the neigh-bors chat-ter all day, be-hind their doors?
Why do you take the troub-le to bake my fav' - rite pie?

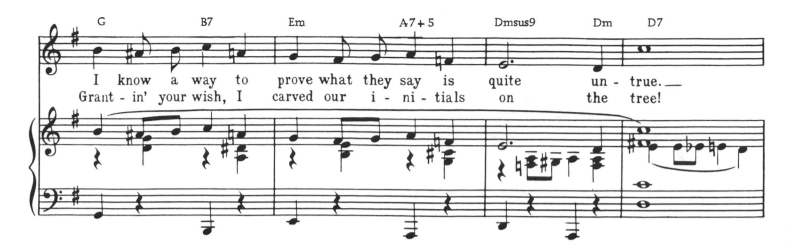

I know a way to prove what they say is quite un - true.___
Grant - in' your wish, I carved our i - ni - tials on the tree!

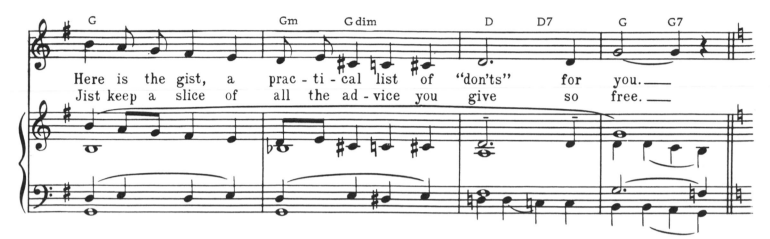

Here is the gist, a prac - ti - cal list of "don'ts" for you.___
Jist keep a slice of all the ad - vice you give so free.___

REFRAIN

Don't throw___ bou - quets at me___ Don't please___
Don't praise___ my charm too much___ Don't look___

___ my folks too much___ Don't laugh___ at my
___ so vane with me___ Don't stand___ in the

jokes too much____ Peo - ple will say we're in love! ____
rain with me ____ Peo - ple will say we're in love! ____

Don't sigh ____ and gaze at me ____
Don't take ____ my arm too much ____

Your sighs ____ are so like mine ____ Your eyes ____
Don't keep ____ your hand in mine ____ Your hand ____

must-n't glow like mine ____ Peo - ple will say we're in
feels so grand in mine ____ Peo - ple will say we're in

LOVE ME OR LEAVE ME

Screenplay: Daniel Fuchs & Isobel Lennart
Produced by: Joe Pasternak for MGM
Directed by: Charles Vidor
Choreography: Alex Romero
Photography: Arthur Arling (Eastman Color; CinemaScope)
Cast: Doris Day, James Cagney, Cameron Mitchell, Robert Keith, Tom Tully, Claude Stroud, Harry Bellaver, Richard Gaines, Joe Pasternak
Songs: "It All Depends on You" (Ray Henderson-B.G. DeSylva, Lew Brown); "You Made Me Love You" (James Monaco-Joe McCarthy); "Everybody Loves My Baby" (Spencer Williams-Jack Palmer); "Sam the Old Accordion Man" (Walter Donaldson); "Shaking the Blues Away" (Irving Berlin); "Ten Cents a Dance" (Richard Rodgers-Lorenz Hart); "I'll Never Stop Loving You" (Nicholas Brodszky-Sammy Cahn); "At Sundown" (Donaldson); "Love Me or Leave Me" (Donaldson-Gus Kahn)
Released: May 1955; 122 minutes

Temporarily freed from her accustomed ginger-peachy girl-next-door roles, Doris Day starred in the first Hollywood biography offering a view of a singer's life that was not excessively sentimentalized or glamorized. *Love Me or Leave Me* tells the story of torch singer Ruth Etting who, beginning as a dime-a-dance hostess, goes on to win fame in nightclubs, the *Ziegfeld Follies*, and movies (though in real life the singer appeared in only three films). What gives a special edge to the story is the character of Gimp Snyder (memorably played by James Cagney), a brutish, but somehow sympathetic mobster who worships Ruth, uses strongarm methods to clear her path to success ("Whoever I am, kiddo, I'm what makes you tick"), and is ultimately cuckolded by his beloved. But producer Joe Pasternak, long associated with family-style musicals, made sure to tack on a happy ending. After Gimp has served time for shooting (but not killing) Ruth's accompanist and lover (Cameron Mitchell), all three are reunited at the opening of Snyder's new nightclub. *Love Me or Leave Me* helped pave the way for such other attempts at a more realistic approach to show-business biographies as *I'll Cry Tomorrow* (Susan Hayworth as Lillian Roth), *The Joker Is Wild* (Frank Sinatra as Joe E. Lewis) and *The Helen Morgan Story* (Ann Blyth with Gogi Grant's singing voice).

CSP ST. MGM/UA VC.

1955

Love Me or Leave Me

FROM LOVE ME OR LEAVE ME

Lyrics by GUS KAHN
Music by WALTER DONALDSON

PETE KELLY'S BLUES

Screenplay: Richard L. Breen
Producer-director: Jack Webb for Warner
    Bros.
Photography: Hal Rosson (WarnerColor;
    CinemaScope)
Cast: Jack Webb, Janet Leigh, Edmond
    O'Brien, Peggy Lee, Andy Devine, Lee
    Marvin, Ella Fitzgerald, Martin Milner, Jayne
    Mansfield, Mort Marshall, Matty Matlock,
    George Van Epps, Nick Fatool, Snub Pollard
Songs: "Sugar" (Maceo Pinkard-Sidney
    Mitchell, Edna Alexander); "Somebody
    Loves Me" (George Gershwin-B.G. DeSylva,
    Ballard MacDonald); "Bye Bye Blackbird"
    (Ray Henderson-Mort Dixon); "What Can I
    Say After I Say I'm Sorry?" (Walter
    Donaldson, Abe Lyman); "He Needs Me" (Arthur Hamilton); "Sing a
    Rainbow" (Hamilton); "Pete Kelly's Blues" (Ray Heindorf-Sammy
    Cahn)
Released: July 1955; 95 minutes

Jack Webb and Peggy Lee.

Best known as the frozen-faced detective in the television series
Dragnet, Jack Webb (with his cornet playing dubbed by Dick
Cathcart) appears in this musical melodrama as a frozen-faced jazz
bandleader fronting Pete Kelly's Big Seven (actually Matty Matlock's
Dixielanders) in a 1927 Kansas City speakeasy. The club's owner, a
sadistic bootlegger (Edmond O'Brien) trying to strong-arm his way into
the talent agency business, is also instrumental in the band hiring has-
been vocalist Peggy Lee (giving an unusually dramatic performance),
who sings nine of the 12 songs (the other three are sung by Ella
Fitzgerald). The movie was inspired by a 1951 radio show of the same
name, in which Cathcart had led the Matlock group.

Decca (Lee, Fitzgerald LP). Warner VC.

1955

Bye Bye Blackbird
FROM PETE KELLY'S BLUES

Lyric by MORT DIXON
Music by RAY HENDERSON

Moderately

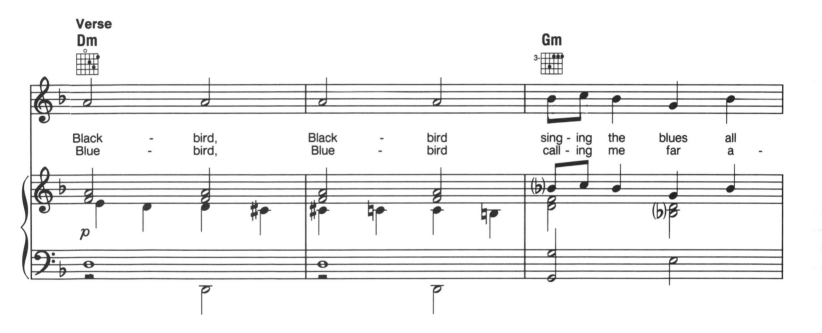

Verse

Black - bird, Black - bird sing - ing the blues all
Blue - bird, Blue - bird call - ing me far a -

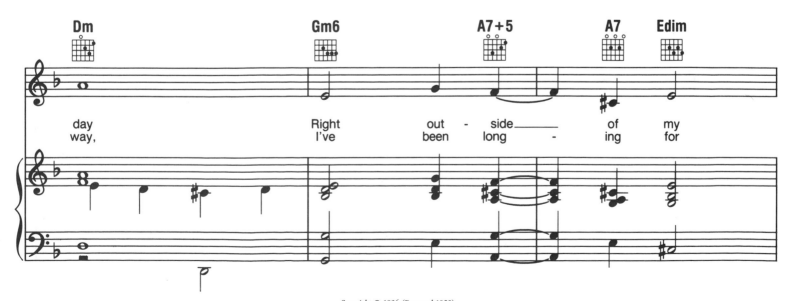

day Right out - side of my
way, I've been long - ing for

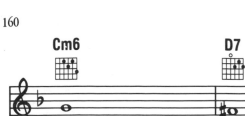

stand me, Oh what hard luck sto-ries they all

hand me; Make my bed and light the light,

I'll ar - rive late to-night, black - bird_____ bye

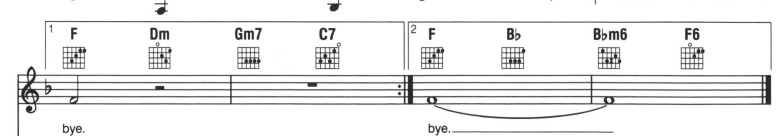

bye. bye._____